IMPACT Intervention Year 3

Stephen Monaghan and Melissa Blackwood

Published by Keen Kite Books
An imprint of HarperCollins*Publishers* Ltd
The News Building
1 London Bridge Street
London
SE1 9GF

Text and design © 2017 Keen Kite Books, an imprint of HarperCollins*Publishers* Ltd

10 9 8 7 6 5 4 3 2 1

ISBN 9780008238452

The author asserts their moral right to be identified as the author of this work.

Any educational institution that has purchased one copy of this publication may make duplicate copies for use exclusively within that institution. Permission does not extend to reproduction, storage in a retrieval system or transmission in any form or by any means – electronic, mechanical, photocopying, recording or otherwise – of duplicate copies for lending, renting or selling to any other user or institution without the prior consent, in writing, of the Publisher.

British Library Cataloguing in Publication Data

A catalogue record for this publication is available from the British Library.

Authors: Stephen Monaghan and Melissa Blackwood
Contributor: Charlotte Monaghan
Commissioning Editors: Shelley Teasdale and Michelle l'Anson
Project Manager: Fiona Watson
Editor: Becki Adlard
Internal design and illustrations: QBS Learning
Production: Lyndsey Rogers

HarperCollins
PUBLISHERS
200
Since 1817

Introduction

Impact Intervention is a new series of resources created by teachers and aimed at teaching assistants, classroom assistants, NQTs and time-strapped teachers.

The books include tried and tested ready-to-go activities that are intended for use with small groups of pupils to help scaffold learning.

The resources can be used to deliver pre-teach sessions, booster interventions or breakout sessions after lessons to pick up pupils who are struggling to achieve a learning outcome.

Impact Intervention can be dipped into as needed and used with minimal preparation.

The books contain:
- standalone sessions with activities that focus on an achievable part of a learning objective
- content that has been broken down into small steps so that it is easy to follow and deliver
- activities that can be easily implemented in a 15–20-minute session without the need to read through lots of information in advance
- probing questions, prompts and key checks to help assess pupils' knowledge and understanding
- support and extension ideas.

Each title in the series contains content that is robust, age-appropriate and adheres to the standard of the KS1 / KS2 English and maths programmes of study.

Contents

IMPACT Intervention
Maths Activities

Partitioning challenge

Strand: Number – number and place value

Learning objective: To recognise the place value of each digit in a three-digit number.

You will need: 0–9 dice, Dienes, Numicon or Lego, whiteboard, whiteboard pens

1. **Say:** *I have a problem for you today that I bet you can't solve.*

2. Roll three 0–9 dice to generate a three-digit number. Write the number (e.g. 346) on a whiteboard, place the whiteboard flat on the table and place the Dienes/Numicon/Lego (in an unlabelled place value chart drawn on the whiteboard) incorrectly (i.e. **not** three hundreds, four tens and six ones). **Ask:** *Is this correct? Why not? Do we have the correct amount of hundreds? Tens? Ones? Do we need more or less?*

3. Encourage the pupils to explain their thoughts. (Steer their thinking to there being the incorrect number of hundreds, tens and/or ones.)

4. Partition the number in expanded form (e.g. 346 = 300 + 40 + 6) or:

300 + 40 + 6

5. **Say:** *The last part of your challenge today is to roll three dice and create your own three-digit number. Then see if you can partition it for me.*

Key checks: Can the pupils partition numbers? Are they using the key vocabulary tens, ones and hundreds?

Extension: Pupils partition three-digit numbers in different ways, e.g.:

346: 300 + 40 + 6   300 + 30 + 16   330 + 16

Support: Pupils partition smaller numbers to start with. Once they demonstrate understanding through clear explanations, using key vocabulary, move on to higher values.

Investigating inequalities

Strand: Number – number and place value

Learning objective: To compare numbers up to 1000.

You will need: whiteboards, whiteboard pens, cubes, Dienes or multi-based arithmetic blocks, 0–9 dice

1. Write the numbers 256 and 265 on the whiteboard.

2. **Ask:** *Which is the biggest number? How do you know? Can you show me how you know?*

3. Draw attention to using place value knowledge to compare digits and the whole number. The pupils may use a drawing here or some of the hands-on equipment suggested above; for example, pupils draw the < or > signs then place the Dienes inside to show how they compare.

4. Write this inequality on the board together: 256 < 265 and 265 > 256.

5. Show these inequalities using the equipment suggested above.

6. **Say together:** *256 is less than 265 and 265 is more than 256.*

7. Write the following on the board below the previous inequalities 445_____ 445. **Ask:** *What would we say if we had the numbers 445 and 445?*

8. Explain that we would say *445 is the same as 445 or 445 is equal to 445.* Ask a pupil to draw the symbol = on the board between the two numbers to complete the number sentence.

9. Ask the pupils to roll dice to generate two three-digit numbers to compare. Ask them to write number sentences using the <, > and = symbols.

Key checks: Do the pupils know what the symbols < and > mean? Are they using the language of more than, less than, equal to?

Extension: Ask pupils to tackle some balancing problems, e.g.

45 + 8 < _____

_____ > 12 + 9

Support: Pupils work first with two-digit numbers to build confidence. When moving on to three-digit numbers, ensure the hundreds are different and focus attention on the hundreds position. Once pupils are more confident with three-digit numbers, progress to using the same hundreds digit, but different tens and units.

Count up

Strand: Number – number and place value

Learning objective: To count from 0 in multiples of 10, 50 and 100.

You will need: 0–9 die, 1–12 die, 1–16 die, whiteboard, whiteboard pen, number line, 100 square

1. **Say:** *Today we will be counting up in fifties and hundreds.*

2. **Ask:** *Do you know your multiplication tables for 5 and 10?*

3. As a group, count out the 5 and 10 multiplication tables using a 100 square.

4. **Say:** *Counting in fifties and hundreds is very similar to counting in fives and tens.*

5. Draw a place value chart on the whiteboard:

    Th   H   T   O

6. **Say:** *Counting in fifties is ten times bigger than counting in fives and counting in hundreds is ten times bigger than counting in tens.* Show this on the place value chart:

Th	H	T	O		Th	H	T	O
			5				1	0
		5	0			1	0	0

7. **Say:** *We need a 0 as a place holder in the ones place when counting with fifties and hundreds.* Write the number sentences on the whiteboard to show this (e.g. 5 × 5 = 25; 5 × 50 = 250).

8. Roll the 0–9 die and use the number it lands on, for example 8, multiplying it by 10.

9. **Say:** *10 × 8 = 80, so 10 × 80 must equal 800.* Show this on the place value chart.

10. Repeat with several more examples.

11. Get pupils to roll the 0–9 die and repeat with other numbers.

12. Chant in hundreds with the pupils (100, 200, 300, 400…).

13. Repeat in fifties (50, 100, 150, 200, 250…).

Key checks: Can pupils count in multiples of fives and tens? Can pupils explain the link between fives and fifties, as well as tens and hundreds? Can they link to place value and multiplying numbers by ten?

Extension: Encourage the pupils to use 1–12 or 1–16 dice to create larger numbers (e.g. 100 × 16 = 1600). **Ask:** *If you know 6 × 50 = 300, can you use this to help you work out 60 × 5?*

Support: Revise counting in fives and tens. Show the connection between the fives and fifties, followed by tens and hundreds. Provide a number line that is marked in fifties and hundreds up to 1000.

Count on and count back

Strand: Number – number and place value

Learning objective: To find 10 or 100 more or less than a given number.

You will need: three 0–9 dice, whiteboard, whiteboard pen, Dienes, 100 square/ number line

1. **Say:** *Today we will be counting in tens and hundreds.* **Ask:** *Can we do this already?*

2. As a group, chant the multiplication tables for 10 and 100 together.

3. Once you have established that the pupils can count in tens and hundreds, move on to the next step. **Say:** *We are going to count in tens and hundreds from different numbers, not just our multiplication tables.*

4. Roll the three dice to generate a number (e.g. 346) and write it on the whiteboard.

5. **Ask:** *Can you count on in tens from this number? What would the next number be?* The pupils should respond with the answer of 356. If not, show this on a number line and count on ten together as a group.

6. Count together as a group and add on 10 each time (e.g. 356, 366, 376, 386). Provide opportunities to cross hundreds (e.g. 479, 489, 499, 509) and to count back in tens, crossing hundreds (e.g. 432, 422, 412, 402, 392).

7. **Ask:** *Can you count on in hundreds from the number we generated earlier?* Count together (e.g. 346, 446). Repeat with other numbers.

Key checks: Are pupils accurately counting in tens and hundreds? Can pupils cross the hundreds boundary?

Extension: Write a number (e.g. 427) and ask the pupils to find four ways of reaching that number counting in tens and hundreds. They should be counting on and counting back.

Support: Allow pupils to use practical apparatus such as Dienes before using more abstract items such as a 100 square/number line. Use a different colour for the digit that is changing each time. Count in multiples of 10 and 100 first, then use a 100 square to demonstrate counting in multiples of 10 from numbers that are not multiples of 10 (e.g. 24, 34, 44, 54). Cross the 100 barrier once confident and move on to counting on in hundreds.

The power of estimation

Strand: Number – number and place value

Learning objective: To use knowledge of rounding to make estimates.

You will need: whiteboards, whiteboard pens, Dienes

1. **Say:** *Today we will be using our knowledge of place value to help us estimate. Does anyone remember what estimate means?*

2. **Say:** *To estimate is to find an answer or a value that is close enough to the right answer but is not exact.*

3. **Say:** *We are going to use our estimating powers to help us with tricky calculations.*

4. Write 77 + 98 = ____ on the whiteboard.

5. **Say:** *This could be a tricky calculation, but we can use our estimating powers to get an 'almost' answer.*

6. **Say:** *Rounding makes the numbers easier to add.* In this example, *we can round the numbers to the nearest ten. When we round, if the ones value is 1, 2, 3 or 4, we round down and if the ones value is 5, 6, 7, 8 or 9 we round up.* Use Dienes to explore this.

7. **Ask:** *What number could we round 77 to? What is the nearest 10?* (80) *How about 98?* (100) Use Dienes to explore this.

8. Write 80 + 100 on the board. **Ask:** *What is 80 + 100?* (180)

9. **Say:** *So the answer to our original question, 77 + 98, should be around 180.*

10. As a group, check the answer to the original problem using addition methods the pupils know.

11. Repeat this with several different questions.

Key checks: Do the pupils fully understand the term 'estimate'? Are they able to round numbers to the nearest 10? Do they know when to round up and when to round down?

Extension: Pupils estimate in hundreds (e.g. 345 + 283; 350 + 280 = 630).

Support: Provide pupils with Dienes equipment so that they can physically see the addition of the tens and use estimation to find the answer. **Say:** *If we round 82 to 80 and 93 to 90 we can count how many groups of tens there are (17). 17 tens are 170. So the answer must be around 170.*

Less or more than?

Strand: Number – number and place value

Learning objective: To find 10 or 100 more or less than a given number.

You will need: three 0–9 dice, whiteboard, whiteboard pen, number line, 100 square

1. **Say:** *Today we will be learning about ten more than and less than and one hundred more than and less than a number.*

2. **Ask:** *Can you count in tens and hundreds already?*

3. As a group, chant in tens (10, 20, 30, 40…) and hundreds (100, 200, 300, 400…).

4. Roll the three dice to generate a number (e.g. 247). **Ask:** *What is ten more than this number? What is ten less? Can you show me how you know?* Pupils could show you using a place value chart and referring to the tens place:

H	T	O
2	4	7
2	5	7
2	3	7

5. **Ask:** *What is 100 more than this number? What is 100 less? Can you show me how you know?* Encourage pupils to use a place value chart and to manipulate the hundreds digit.

H	T	O
2	4	7
3	4	7
1	4	7

6. Ask the pupils to repeat with other numbers by rolling the three dice.

Key checks: Ensure the pupils can count in tens and hundreds first.

Extension: Write some examples that are wrong and ask pupils to check them and explain why the calculation is incorrect, e.g. 407 – 10 = 497.

Support: Use easier numbers – number bonds to 10 and 100, e.g. for 170:

10 more = 180, 10 less = 160
100 more = 270, 100 less = 70

Allow pupils to use a 0–1000 number line to help them.

May the 4s be with you

Strand: Number – number and place value

Learning objective: To count on in multiples of four from a given number.

You will need: dice (0–6 for ones and 0–9 for tens), whiteboard, whiteboard pen, number line, 100 square

1. **Say:** *Today, we will be counting in fours.*

2. **Ask:** *Can you count in fours already?*

3. Show the pupils a 100 square and, as a group, count in multiples of 4. Make the link to the multiplication table for 2 and how the pupils will only say every other multiple: 2, 4, 6, 8, 10, 12.

4. Once you have established that the pupils can count in fours, move on to the next step.

5. **Say:** *We are going to count in fours from a different number, not just our multiplication tables.*

6. Roll two dice to generate a number (e.g. 45). Write this number on the whiteboard.

7. **Ask:** *Can you count in fours from this number? What would the next number be?* The pupils should respond with the answer of 49. If not, show this on a number line and count on four together as a group.

8. Count together as a group and add on four each time (49, 53, 57, 61, 65).

9. Repeat with other numbers (use the dice to generate starting numbers).

Key checks: Make sure the pupils can count in fours first.

Extension: Pupils generalise whether an answer will be odd or even using knowledge that:

even + even = even

odd + even = odd

Support: Practise counting in multiples of four first. Can they show the pattern on a number line? Pupils use a 100 square/number line to help them answer.

Awesome addition

Strand: Number – addition and subtraction

Learning objective: To add a three-digit number and ones.

You will need: whiteboard, whiteboard pens, 0–9 dice, Dienes

1. **Say:** *Today we are going to do some awesome addition.*

2. **Ask:** *What is addition?*

3. **Say:** *Addition is finding the calculation, or total, by joining two or more numbers together.*

4. **Say:** *Today we will be adding a one-digit number to a three-digit number.*

5. Write 312 on the board and roll a 0–9 die (e.g. it might land on 7).

6. **Ask:** *What is 312 add 7?* Pupils respond.

7. Draw a number line on the whiteboard and show the pupils 312 + 7 by counting on.

8. Count on together: *313, 314, 315, 316, 317, 318, 319. 312 add 7 equals 319.*

9. Repeat with different numbers, including crossing the tens barrier.

Key checks: Make sure the pupils can add a one-digit number to two digits first, including crossing the tens boundary.

Extension: Pupils add a two-digit number to a three-digit number, e.g. 517 + 16 = 533. Pupils generalise whether the answer will be odd or even using knowledge that:

even + even = even

odd + even = odd

Support: Pupils practise adding one-digit numbers to two-digit numbers, including crossing over the tens barrier. Once confident, move them on to a one-digit number being added to a three-digit number.

Superb subtraction

Strand: Number – addition and subtraction

Learning objective: To subtract a one-digit number from two- and three-digit numbers.

You will need: whiteboard, whiteboard pens, 0–9 die, Dienes, number line, 100 square, objects

1. **Say:** *Today we are going to do some superb subtraction.*

2. **Ask:** *What is subtraction?* **Say:** *Subtraction is taking one thing from another.*

3. **Say:** *Today we will be subtracting a one-digit number from larger numbers.*

4. Write the number 68 and draw a number line on the whiteboard.

5. Roll a 0–9 die to generate a number to take away (e.g. 5).

6. **Ask:** *What is 68 subtract 5? How do you know? Can you show me on your board?*

7. Write 68 at the end of the number line and, as a group, draw the jumps backwards as you subtract.

8. Count backwards together: *67, 66, 65, 64, 63.*

9. Repeat using the same method using three-digit numbers once the pupils are confident with two digits.

Key checks: Can the pupils subtract through the tens barrier and provide explanations as to why and how they found their answer?

Extension: Pupils generalise whether the answer will be odd or even using knowledge that:

even – even = even

odd – even = odd

Support: Help pupils to show understanding of subtraction using their number bonds to 20. Then progress on to larger two-digit numbers. Pupils explain their thinking using a number line, 100 square or objects. Emphasise explaining using key vocabulary and tools.

Block addition

Strand: Number – addition and subtraction

Learning objective: To add a three-digit number and tens.

You will need: whiteboard, whiteboard pens, Dienes/base 10 (100s, 10s and 1s), 100 square

1. **Ask:** *Who can add a two-digit number to a three-digit number?* Ask pupils to explain how they might do it and write up any useful vocabulary on the board.

2. Write 443 + 40 on the whiteboard. Show this addition using the base 10 blocks:

   443   + 40 =   483

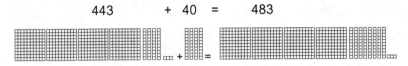

3. Write 236 + 80 and use the base 10 blocks to show the calculation.

4. **Say:** *When the tens blocks get to 100 we can use the 100 block.* To show this, place 10 tens blocks next to a 100 block so that the pupils can visualise this.

5. Ask the pupils to repeat this activity with different calculations.

Key checks: Can the pupils identify which blocks are used for ones, tens and hundreds?

Extension: Give pupils problems that cross the tens and hundreds barriers.

Support: On a 100 square, pupils add tens to two-digit numbers, e.g. 12 + 10 = 22. Repeat, adding 10 to various numbers and then progress to adding 20, 30, 40, etc. Pupils discuss how to use a 100 square when adding 10.

Big block addition

Strand: Number – addition and subtraction

Learning objective: To add a three-digit number and hundreds.

You will need: whiteboard, whiteboard pens, Dienes/base 10 (100s, 10s and 1s)

1. **Ask:** *Who can add a three-digit number to another three-digit number?* Ask pupils to explain how they might do it and write up any useful vocabulary on the board.

2. Write 125 + 500 on the whiteboard. Show this addition using the base 10 blocks:

125   +   500   =   625

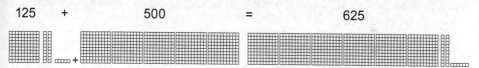

3. Write 345 + 600 and use the base 10 blocks to show the calculation.

4. Ask the pupils to repeat this activity with different calculations.

Key checks: Can the pupils identify which blocks are used for ones, tens and hundreds?

Extension: Give pupils problems that cross the tens and hundreds barrier.

Support: Pupils add tens to a three-digit number and then progress to adding one hundred. Pupils focus on the correct place value position to look at and use Dienes equipment to show the number enlarging. Do not cross over the thousands barrier. Allow the pupils to use tens to begin with to build their confidence.

Powerful partitioning

Strand: Number – addition and subtraction

Learning objective: To partition and recombine to add.

You will need: whiteboard, whiteboard pens, Dienes/base 10 (100s, 10s and 1s)

1. **Say:** *Today we will be partitioning numbers to add. Let's try to add 17 and 14.*

2. Write the number 17 on the whiteboard. **Ask:** *How do we make 17? Can you show me using the equipment on the table?*

3. Encourage the pupils to use the base 10 blocks to make 17. **Ask:** *Can you explain what you've done?*

4. Write 10 + 7 = 17 on the whiteboard. Demonstrate how to use the base 10 blocks to complete this addition.

10   7   17

5. Then ask the pupils to partition 14 into tens and ones.

10   4   14

6. **Say:** *Now that we have partitioned the two numbers we can add them together more easily.* Ask the pupils to group the tens and ones (this could be done on a whiteboard with the headings T and O).

7. **Ask:** *What happens when we get to ten ones?* (we exchange it for a ten)

8. Ask the pupils to repeat with different numbers.

Key checks: Can the pupils identify which blocks are used for ones, tens and hundreds?

Extension: Ask pupils to partition three-digit numbers in different ways:

866:   800 + 66   800 + 60 + 6   800 + 30 + 36.

Support: Allow pupils to work with smaller numbers to begin with (e.g. 15 = 10 + 5) and use the equipment to help them demonstrate partitioning.

Partitioning for subtraction

Strand: Number – addition and subtraction

Learning objective: To partition and recombine to subtract.

You will need: whiteboards, whiteboard pens, Dienes/base 10 blocks (10s and 1s), 100 square, number line

1. Write 19 – 6 on the whiteboard. **Ask:** *What is 19 – 6? Can you show me the calculation using the equipment on the table?* Encourage the pupils to use the base 10 equipment to show the calculation.

2. Write 19 – 6 = 13 on the whiteboard, then write 29 – 16 = 13.

3. Explain that this can be written like this to break the calculation down into more manageable chunks – subtract the ones first, then the tens:

   29 – 16   (16 = one ten (10) and six ones (6))

   Stage 1   29 – 6 = 23

   Stage 2   23 – 10 = 13

4. Use a 100 square/number line to show the subtraction taking place.

5. Write 142 – 32 on the whiteboard and repeat:

   142 – 32   (32 = three tens (30), two ones (2))

   Stage 1   142 – 30 = 112

   Stage 2   112 – 2 = 110

6. Ask pupils to repeat with different numbers.

Key checks: Do the pupils know how to work through each stage?

Extension: Allow pupils to move onto subtracting three-digit numbers from other three-digit numbers.

Support: Pupils subtract two-digit numbers from two- and then three-digit numbers with 0 in the ones place, e.g. 20 – 15 = ? 140 – 12 = ? Use Dienes equipment to partition the number and a 100 square to demonstrate subtraction.

Column kings and queens

Strand: Number – addition and subtraction

Learning objective: To use formal written methods of columnar addition.

You will need: whiteboards, whiteboard pens, Dienes, number line, 100 square

1. **Ask:** *How else can we say add?* Write any alternatives on the board. *Can we add more than two numbers together? When might you use addition?*

2. **Say:** *We are going to answer 24 + 12, but we are going to set our calculation out using columns, like this:*

$$\begin{array}{r} \text{T O} \\ 14 \\ +12 \\ \hline \end{array}$$

3. **Say:** *We have put the numbers in columns so that we know which are tens and which are ones.* **Ask:** *How many tens in 24? (2) How many ones in 24? (4) How many tens in 12? (1) How many ones in 12? (2).*

4. As a group, work through the question. **Say:** *4 ones add 2 ones equals 6 ones and 2 tens add 1 ten equals 3 tens.* (You may want to use the Dienes equipment to show the tens and ones.)

5. Repeat this with other addition questions such as 16 + 15. When you get to crossing the tens barrier, **say:** *We exchange 10 ones for 1 ten and write it in the tens place below the total line so that we remember to add it to the tens.*

$$\begin{array}{r} \text{T O} \\ 16 \\ +15 \\ \hline 31 \\ {\scriptstyle 1} \end{array}$$

Key checks: Are the pupils starting with the ones and moving to the left? Make sure the pupils put any tens or hundreds made from adding underneath the correct column and remember to include them as they continue the addition. Are they writing the numbers in the correct columns (H, T or O)?

Extension: Allow pupils to calculate with more numbers that cross the tens or hundreds barriers.

Support: Pupils use Dienes to aid partitioning and counting in tens and ones. If adding two-digit numbers is tricky, add a single-digit using the column method and then progress to two digits, but NOT crossing the tens barrier. Pupils use a number line or 100 square to double check their thinking.

Subtracting columns

Strand: Number – addition and subtraction

Learning objective: To use formal written methods of columnar subtraction.

You will need: Dienes, cubes, number line, 100 square

1. **Ask:** *How else can we say subtract?* Write any ideas on the board. *Can we subtract in any order? When might you use subtraction?* Remind pupils that the largest number will go on top in columnar subtraction.

2. **Say:** *We are going to answer 28 – 11, but we are going to set our calculation out using columns, like this:*

   ```
   T O
   2 8
   - 1 1
   ─────
   ```

3. **Say:** *We have put the numbers in columns so that we know which are tens and which are ones.* **Ask:** *How many tens in 28?* (2) *How many ones in 28?* (8) Repeat with 11 (1 ten and 1 one). As a group, work through the question. **Say:** *8 ones take away 1 one equals 7 ones and 2 tens take away 1 ten is 1 ten.* (You may want to use the Dienes equipment to show the tens and ones.)

4. Repeat with other subtraction questions such as 33 – 15. When there are not enough ones to subtract from, we can exchange one of the tens for 10 ones. Show the pupils this using cubes and exchange 1 ten for 10 ones.

   ```
   T O
   2 1
   3̸ 3
   - 1 5
   ─────
   ```

   In this example, **Say:** *3 ones is not enough ones to take 5 ones from, so we need to exchange one ten for 10 ones, so 33 becomes 20 and 13 ones. 13 – 5 is 8. 2 tens take away 1 ten is 1 ten, so the difference is 18.*

Key checks: Do pupils know to record any exchanges? Do they place the digits in the correct columns? Are they starting with the ones column and working to the left?

Extension: Write two number facts for the bar model below:

245	
95	150

Support: Pupils use Dienes to aid partitioning and subtracting. Subtract a single-digit number using the column method and then progress to two-digit numbers, but without crossing the tens barrier. Supply a number line or 100 square for checking.

Crack the code

Strand: Number – multiplication and division

Learning objective: To solve problems, including missing number problems, using number facts, place value and multiplication and division.

You will need: whiteboards, whiteboard pens, multiplication grid, number line, Dienes

1. **Say:** *Today we are going to use our knowledge of multiplication tables to solve problems and crack mathematical codes!*

2. Write 5 × ⬤ = 20 on the whiteboard. **Ask:** *Can anyone crack the code and work out what number the circle represents?* (4)

3. **Ask:** *How do we know the circle represents four? Show me how you know.* Pupils should respond that they know that five multiplied by four equals twenty. Ask them to count in fives to prove this.

4. Write ⬛ ÷ 4 = 5 and **Ask:** *What number does the square represent?* (20)

5. **Ask:** *How do we know the square represents 20? Show me how you know.* Pupils should respond that if five multiplied by four equals twenty then twenty divided by four will equal five.

6. Write 3 △ 5 = 15 **Ask:** *What does the triangle represent?* (×) *Show me how you know.* Pupils should respond that they know that three multiplied by five equals fifteen. Ask them to count in threes to prove this.

7. Repeat these activities with the multiplication tables that the pupils are familiar with and listen for use of key vocabulary.

Key checks: Do pupils know their 2, 5, 10, 4, 3 and 8 multiplication tables? Can the pupils complete the questions when the symbols are in a variety of positions?

Extension: Pupils write their own problems for others to solve. They must show their working to ensure it is a sensible/correct answer before sharing. Pupils attempt problems with two codes to crack (e.g. ⬛ ÷ 5 = △).

Support: Pupils investigate multiples of two, five and 10 before moving on to fours and threes. Use a multiplication grid or a number line to check their thinking once they have demonstrated understanding linked to key vocabulary.

Double it

Strand: Number – multiplication and division

Learning objective: To know doubles of multiples of 10 to 100.

You will need: Dienes equipment (tens and ones), whiteboards, whiteboard pens, cubes, 0–9 dice, cubes, counters, number line, 100 square

. **Say:** *Today we will be using our knowledge of doubling smaller numbers to help us double bigger numbers.*

. Write 3 on the whiteboard and **Ask:** *What is double three? Show me using the equipment.*

. **Say:** *If we know double three is six, what is double 30? Can anyone show me using the equipment?* Establish that 30 is ten times bigger than 3 so double 30 must be 10 times bigger than double 3, so the answer is 10 times bigger, and use Dienes to represent this.

. Repeat with 4 and 40, 8 and 80.

. **Ask:** *Can you write both answers?* (8 doubled is 16 and 80 doubled is 160)

. Ask pupils to challenge each other. **Say:** *Challenge your partner. Roll a die to generate a number for your partner to double and multiply by 10.*

Key checks: Ensure the pupils know the double of single-digit numbers before they start to double multiples of 10.

Extension: Pupils attempt to double harder numbers (e.g. 25: double 20 is 40 and double 5 is 10; add together to make 50). Pupils show their thinking and offer reasoning. Can they offer any advice to others? How can they use this method when doubling 100 numbers?

Support: Provide pupils with cubes/Dienes, counters so that they can see the doubling taking place and count the total. Give pupils a number line or 100 square to help them see the doubling.

Super zero

Strand: Number – multiplication and division

Learning objective: To multiply and divide by ten using zero as a placeholder.

You will need: whiteboards, whiteboard pens, written place value grids

1. **Ask:** *Does anyone know why the digit zero is so special?*

2. **Say:** *Zero can be used as a placeholder. For example, without a zero, 40 would look like four! A zero is needed to let people know that there are four tens not four ones.* Demonstrate on the board (see right).

H	T	O
	4	0
	4	

3. **Say:** *When we multiply by 10, each digit becomes ten times bigger in value, so each digit now needs to be recorded one place to the left. Remember to put a zero in the ones column to 'hold' the digits in their correct place.* Draw the following on the board:

H	T	O
	2	0
2	0	0

20 × 10 = 200

←——————————

4. Ask for one pupil to volunteer to be zero. **Say:** *I need a volunteer to be zero. Your job is to help out or disappear when needed. Everyone else needs to help zero decide when he/she is needed or not.*

5. Write HTO on separate whiteboards on the floor (place value grid).

6. Ask one pupil to write 4 on their whiteboard and place it in the correct column on the floor (O).

7. Write 4 × 10 on the whiteboard. **Ask:** *What will happen to the four when we multiply it by 10?* (it becomes 10 times bigger, so we need to record it in the tens place) *Does the ones column stay empty? What happens? Why?* The pupil with the '0' should step up and place their number in the correct column on the floor.

8. Ask the pupils to make a number sentence together (e.g. 7 × 10 = 70). At this point, the pupil who is zero should pop up next to the 7, which will make the 7 ten times bigger to make 70.

Say: *When we divide by 10, each digit becomes 10 times smaller, so it is recorded one place to the right.*

H	T	O
	2	0
		2

$$20 \div 10 = 2$$

→

0. Write $60 \div 10$ on the whiteboard. Ask the pupils to be 6 and 10. 6 and zero will be next to each other and then the zero will disappear.

1. Repeat this to check pupils' understanding.

Key checks: Do pupils recognise what is happening to the number when we multiply or divide by 10?

Extension: Encourage pupils to work in the hundreds.

Support: Provide pupils with a written place value grid to help them move numbers. Focus on multiplication first. Discuss and demonstrate the importance of the place value holder when dividing. **Ask:** *What happens if we do not use it? How does it change our answer?*

Multiplication war

Strand: Number – multiplication and division

Learning objective: To recall and use multiplication and division facts for the 3, 4 and 8 multiplication tables.

You will need: whiteboards, whiteboard pens, a deck of cards with picture cards removed or number cards 1–10, a pack of products for each multiplication table

1. **Say:** *Today we will be playing multiplication war with a deck of cards. In this game we have to use our multiplication tables to win the war. There are two battle grounds: Multiplication and Division.*

2. As a group, chant the 3, 4 and 8 multiplication tables. Ensure the pupils know these tables before you begin the game. (This game can be adapted to use the multiplication tables you are focusing on.)

3. **Say:** *I will write either threes, fours or eights on the board. To play the game you need to flip a card and multiply the number on your card by the number on the board. Whoever has the highest product keeps all the players' cards. If you can give me the inverse division problem, you'll get a bonus point!*

4. Play a round using threes as the number on the board. One pupil might draw a six, so they would multiply this by three and their product would be 18, with the inverse 18 divided by 3 equals 6 etc.

5. Repeat with fours and eights.

Key checks: Ensure the pupils know their multiplication tables before they start this game.

Extension: Ask pupils to complete the bar model below:

48					

Support: Pupils investigate twos, fives and tens with cards first. When they are confident with this, remind them of the threes facts. Play the card game for threes. Repeat with fours. Give pupils a times table grid so they can check their answers to build confidence with threes and fours.

Get gridding!

Strand: Number – multiplication and division

Learning objective: To partition into tens and ones to multiply a two-digit number by a one-digit number.

You will need: whiteboards, whiteboard pens, multiplication grids, a 12 × 12 multiplication chart

1. **Ask:** *Who can multiply a number by 10? What do we do to multiply by 10?*
   Say: *We move all the digits one place to the left because each digit becomes ten times bigger and must be positioned in the next column. Remember to put a zero in the ones column as a place holder.*

2. Write 14 × 3 on the whiteboard and **Ask:** *How can we solve this question? The numbers are a bit big and tricky! But I know a way we can do it!*

3. **Ask:** *How do we make 14?* (14 is 10 and 4.) Draw a grid and write in the numbers:

×	10	4
3		

4. **Explain:** *We have partitioned 14 into tens (1) and ones (4) and will multiply each number by 3.*

5. **Explain:** *First we are multiplying 10 by 3, 30.* Write this in the grid:

×	10	4
3	30	

6. *Then move onto your ones and do 3 × 4, which equals 12.* Write this in the grid:

7. **Say:** *Then we add these two together: 30 + 12 = 42. So the answer to 14 × 3 is 42.*

×	10	4
3	30	12

8. Repeat with different questions involving a teen number. Encourage pupils to draw grids and work through each problem as a group.

Key checks: Are the pupils setting their work out correctly? Are the pupils partitioning the two-digit numbers correctly?

Extension: Create multiplication grids with missing numbers, including giving answers but missing out parts of the partitioned question number.

Support: Provide the pupils with a 12 × 12 multiplication chart to support their multiplication. Focus on multiplying by 2, 5, 3, and 4.

Lines of division

Strand: Number – multiplication and division

Learning objective: To divide a two-digit number by a one-digit number.

You will need: whiteboards, whiteboard pens, number lines

1. **Say:** *Today, we will be learning more about division using our multiplication tables knowledge. Division is splitting objects or numbers into equal parts or groups or 'fair sharing'.* Ask for examples of things pupils might share.

2. Write 56 ÷ 4 on the board. **Ask:** *What is the question asking us? How many groups of four can we make from 56? Don't worry, you don't need to know your multiplication table for 4 up to 56. We can work it out.* Draw a number line and **Say:** *We can use a number line to count in fours until we reach 56, like this:*

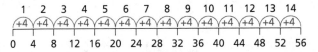

3. **Say:** *Or we could count in groups of four by using our knowledge of the multiplication table for 4.*

4. Establish what multiplication table facts the pupils know. **Say:** *What is 10 multiplied by 4?* (40) *What is 5 multiplied by 4?* (20) *What is 2 multiplied by 4?* (8) **Say:** *We can use our knowledge of multiplication tables to make bigger jumps on the number line, like this:*

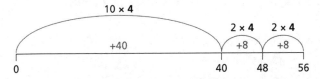

5. Explain that we count the number of jumps and add them up (10 + 2 + 2 = 14). **Say:** *56 ÷ 4 = 14.*

6. Repeat with more questions from appropriate multiplication tables.

Key checks: Ensure the pupils know their multiplication facts to help them group (×10, ×5, ×2).

Extension: Encourage pupils to work with higher numbers (such as 92 ÷ 4) so that they work with 20 times a number (larger jumps).

Support: Provide pupils with a completed number line to support counting using questions linked to multiples of 2, 5, 3 and 4.

Problematic problems

Strand: Number – multiplication and division

Learning objective: To solve two-step word problems using multiplication and division.

You will need: whiteboards, whiteboard pens, number lines, times table squares

1. **Say:** *Today we will be learning how to answer tricky word problems that involve two steps.*

2. Write the following problem on the board: 'A basket holds 10 oranges. Margaret has 12 baskets of oranges. How many oranges does she have in total?'

3. **Ask:** *What are the key bits of information in this question? Is it a multiplication problem or a division problem? How do you know? Show me.*

4. As a group, underline the key parts (10 oranges, 12 baskets, in total).

5. Work through the problem using the grid method on the board:

6. Write: 'She decides to share the oranges between her six friends. How many oranges will they get each?' Underline the important parts and use a number line to solve as a group:

×	10
10	100
2	20

$100 + 20 = 120$

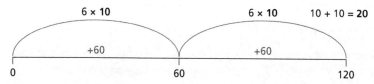

(6 × 20 = 120, 120 divided by 6 = 20, so each friend will get 20 oranges)

7. Repeat with more examples (e.g. An oven can fit 4 bun trays. Each bun tray holds 12 buns. How many buns can be baked in the oven? After they are baked, the buns are shared between 8 shops. How many buns will each shop get?).

Key checks: Are the pupils able to identify the key parts of the question?

Extension: Encourage the pupils to work with harder multiplication tables.

Support: Work with one-step word problems with calculations linked to 2, 5, 3 and 4 multiplication tables. Give pupils multiplication squares to check their answers.

Fractions of quantities

Strand: Number – fractions

Learning objective: To find fractions of quantities.

You will need: whiteboards, whiteboard pens, cubes/shapes

1. **Ask:** *What is a fraction?* Allow pupils to answer. Write any key vocabulary on the board.

2. **Say:** *A fraction is part of a whole. The numerator (top number) tells us how many parts we have and the denominator (bottom number) tells us how many parts the whole is divided into.*

3. **Say:** *Today we are going to find fractions of quantities/amounts. We will start easy and work up to harder ones.*

4. **Ask:** *Using the equipment on the table, can you show me half of 12?* (6)

5. Repeat with quarters (3) and thirds (4). **Ask:** *How does knowing your multiplication facts help you to divide into fractions?*

6. Draw three squares on the board and split them into quarters. **Say:** *Draw this on your board and show me* $\frac{3}{4}$. The pupils may show this in different ways, e.g.

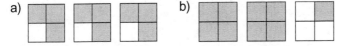

7. Discuss why pupils have used different strategies.

8. Find fractions of quantities using cubes and shapes. Allow pupils to group in appropriate numbers (i.e. group into threes if working in thirds).

Key checks: Are pupils using their multiplication facts to help them? Can they explain why they have chosen to work a certain way?

Extension: Draw six circles on the board and **say:** *This is* $\frac{3}{5}$ *of a bag of marbles. How many marbles will there be altogether in the bag?* (10)

Support: Provide pupils with objects that can be divided into groups to show fractions. Limit quantities to multiples of 2, 3, 4 or 5. Focus on the importance of the denominator to show how many items are in a group. E.g. $\frac{1}{2}$ of 6 means make two equal groups using the six items. This is the same as six divided by two.

Tricky halving

Strand: Number – fractions

Learning objective: To find half of each of the numbers to 30.

You will need: whiteboards, whiteboard pens, counters

1. **Say:** *Today we will be learning more about halving and how to do it confidently.*

2. **Ask:** *Do you know your doubles and half facts? How do you think these facts help you? Let's have a look, using the example half of 17.*

3. Write the number 17 on the whiteboard. **Ask:** *What is the number 17 made up of?* (one ten and a seven or one ten and seven ones) **Say:** *Finding half of 10 is quite easy, but finding half of seven is tricky.*

4. **Say:** *Six is a pretty close double fact to seven. How can we use this to find half of seven? We know that half of six is three and that seven is one more than six, so half of seven would be three with one left over. What happens to that leftover one? We need to split it in half. Write that as a half, $\frac{1}{2}$. So half of seven is $3\frac{1}{2}$.*

5. **Say:** *So we have halved the 7 ones in 17.* **Ask:** *What else do we need to half?* (10). Pupils offer suggestions. **Say:** *So half of 10 is 5.*

6. **Say:** *Five add three and a half is eight and a half. So the answer to half of 17 is eight and a half.*

7. Write $\frac{1}{2}$ of 17 = $8\frac{1}{2}$ on the board.

8. Repeat with other odd numbers between 0 and 30.

Key checks: Can the pupils explain why it is easier to halve even numbers than odd? (i.e. you can create two equal groups with even numbers and cannot with odd numbers unless you half one object)

Extension: Say: *Two boys share three bars of chocolate equally. Two girls share five bars of chocolate equally. Who gets more chocolate? The girls or the boys? Explain why.*

Support: Pupils focus on even numbers less than 10 and move on to even numbers more than 10 once confident. Focus on partitioning two-digit numbers evenly into two groups. Then move onto halving odd numbers below 10. **Ask:** *What did you find? What will happen with odd two-digit numbers? How can you show your thinking?*

What makes one?

Strand: Number – fractions

Learning objective: To count up and down in tenths; to recognise that tenths arise from dividing an object into 10 equal parts and in dividing one-digit numbers or quantities by 10.

You will need: whiteboards, whiteboard pens, 10 cubes/counters, Dienes, a fraction wall

1. **Ask:** *What is the smallest number you can think of? Why is that the smallest number?* **Say:** *Today you will be counting in small units called 'tenths'.*

2. Show the pupils what tenths look like, for example:

$$\frac{1}{10} \qquad \frac{2}{10} \qquad \frac{3}{10} \qquad \frac{4}{10} \qquad \frac{5}{10}$$

3. Elicit which is the numerator and which is the denominator.

4. Show the pupils 10 cubes/counters placed together and explain that this is one whole, one.

5. Split the 10 cubes/counters to represent the tenths. **Say:** *Look, now we have split our whole one into ten equal sections or tenths.*

6. As a group, count from 0 to 1 in tenths: *one-tenth, two-tenths, etc.*

7. **Ask:** *Can you show me $\frac{4}{10}$ on your whiteboard?* Allow pupils time to draw $\frac{4}{10}$ of a whole object on their whiteboards. Ask them to explain what they have done. Repeat with different tenths.

Key checks: Can the pupils tell/demonstrate how many more tenths you would need to make a whole or 1? (e.g. $\frac{4}{10}$ would need $\frac{6}{10}$ to make a whole or 1)

Extension: Pupils create pictorial representations of known fractions.

Support: Pupils use Dienes to show how many hundreds in a thousand, tens in a hundred and ones in ten. Provide a fraction wall so pupils can see how $\frac{10}{10}$ makes a whole. Focus on how to write tenths as a fraction. Ask pupils to show a variety of tenth fractions ($\frac{1}{10}$, $\frac{4}{10}$ or even $\frac{8}{10}$) using the fraction wall.

Fraction vs Fraction

Strand: Number – fractions

Learning objective: To compare fractions with the same denominators.

You will need: whiteboards, whiteboard pens, cubes/counters, fraction wall

1. **Say:** *Today we will be learning more about fractions and how to order them. Can anyone remember the names of the parts of a fraction?*

2. Draw two identical rectangles split into fifths and shade $\frac{2}{5}$ of one and $\frac{4}{5}$ of the other.

3. **Ask:** *Can you name the fractions? Which fraction is larger? How do you know?*

4. **Ask:** *Can you write an inequality to show which is bigger?*

5. Remind pupils of the symbols < and >. Ask pupils to write number sentences comparing $\frac{2}{5}$ and $\frac{4}{5}$ using the symbols ($\frac{2}{5} < \frac{4}{5}$ and $\frac{4}{5} > \frac{2}{5}$).

6. Draw two circles and divide each into quarters. Shade $\frac{1}{4}$ of the first circle and $\frac{3}{4}$ of the second circle. **Say:** *Can you write the number sentences for these fractions?*

7. Repeat with different fractions, eventually moving away from drawing and shading the shapes and just writing the fractions.

8. **Say:** *We're going to play a game called fraction versus fraction. I'm going to say a fraction denominator, for example, quarters, and you have to draw or write a fraction, so that might be $\frac{1}{4}$ or $\frac{2}{4}$ or $\frac{3}{4}$ or $\frac{4}{4}$. Then I'm going to say either largest or smallest. The winner is the person with the largest or smallest fraction.*

9. You could extend the game by **asking:** *Can you work out how many more of a fraction you need to make a whole? What would happen if we added both fractions together? Can you draw it?*

Key checks: Can pupils name the fractions? Do they know what the numerator and denominator are?

Extension: Challenge the pupils to compare fractions with different denominators (e.g. $\frac{2}{4} = \frac{1}{2}$).

Support: Provide pupils with objects that can be divided into groups to show fraction amounts. Limit to quarters, halves, thirds, fifths and tenths. Focus on the importance of the denominator to show the number of equal parts (how many groups) and the numerator to show how many of those groups you have.

Number line fractions

Strand: Number – fractions

Learning objective: To order fractions on a number line.

You will need: whiteboards, whiteboard pens, fraction wall

1. **Say:** *Today we will be learning about how to order fractions on a number line. Can you remember the names of the parts of a fraction?* (numerator and denominator)

2. Write $\frac{1}{6}, \frac{2}{6}, \frac{3}{6}, \frac{4}{6}, \frac{5}{6}, \frac{6}{6}$ in random order around the board.

3. Draw a number line with a 0 and 1 and **ask:** *Can you place these fractions in the correct place on the number line?*

4. **Ask:** *Which fraction should we add to the number line first? Why?* (e.g. $\frac{3}{6}$ because it is a half so it goes in the middle, which is easy to find, or $\frac{6}{6}$ because it is a whole so it goes at the end). As a group, write the fractions in the correct place.

5. Repeat with other fractions with the same denominators.

Key checks: Do the pupils understand numerator and denominator? Can they draw fractions on a whiteboard? Can they write fractions on a number line?

Extension: Pupils order fractions with different denominators (halves, quarters and thirds).

Support: Look at larger fractions first and work to smaller fractions. Provide pupils with a fraction wall chart.

Only compare like for like denominators on the number line first. **Ask:** *Can you see a connection between any fractions? Why do you think this? Can you show me?*

Fraction addition and subtraction

Strand: Number – fractions

Learning objective: To add and subtract fractions with the same denominator within one whole.

You will need: whiteboards, whiteboard pens, fraction walls (that can be cut out)

1. **Say:** *Today we will be learning about how to add and subtract fractions.*

2. **Say:** *To add fractions with the same denominator, we simply add the numerators together. What is the numerator? What does it tell us?* (How many parts we have.)

3. Write an example:

$$\frac{1}{6} + \frac{2}{6} = \frac{3}{6}$$

4. **Say:** *We are only adding the numerators, not the denominators.*

5. **Ask:** *Why would we only add the numerator and not the denominator? What does the denominator tell us?* (How many parts the whole is divided into.)

6. Show what would happen if we added the denominator too:

$$\frac{1}{6} + \frac{2}{6} = \frac{3}{12}$$

7. Show this on a fraction wall:

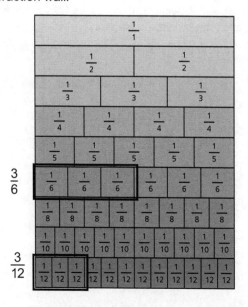

35

8. Discuss how $\frac{3}{6}$ is more than $\frac{3}{12}$. **Ask:** *If this was a pizza, who would get more pizza – the person with $\frac{3}{6}$ or the person with $\frac{3}{12}$?*

9. Once the group understands to add only the numerator, write more addition questions on the board for them to answer.

10. **Say:** *Let's look at subtracting fractions.* **Ask:** *What do you need to remember when subtracting fractions?* (e.g. Only work with the numerator when the denominators are the same.)

11. Write $\frac{4}{6} - \frac{2}{6} =$ **Ask:** *How can we solve this?* Pupils offer written subtraction or pictorial representations.

12. **Ask:** *Why is the denominator 6 and not 0?* Pupils should explain that the question is focused on the numerator and how many sixths are remaining.

13. Repeat with other subtraction questions where the denominator is the same, remembering to refer to quantity of fraction (e.g. $\frac{4}{7} - \frac{1}{7} = \frac{3}{7}$ = three-sevenths).

Key checks: Do the pupils know what the numerator and denominator are? Are they remembering to add just the numerator?

Extension: Write $\frac{}{6} + \frac{}{6} = 1$ and ask the pupils to find as many ways as possible to make the calculation correct (e.g. $\frac{2}{6} + \frac{4}{6} = 1$). Ask pupils to explain their thoughts.

Support: Provide pupils with their own fraction wall chart so they can check their workings. Provide pupils with individual fraction walls to cut out. They should be able to physically cut and move different fractions around to compare them. Pupils should focus on quarters and thirds.

Adding measures

Learning objective: To add lengths (m/cm/mm), mass (kg/g) and volume/capacity (L/mL).

You will need: whiteboards, whiteboard pens, Dienes

. **Ask:** *What do we measure length in?* (mm, cm and m) *What do we measure mass in?* (g and kg) *What do we measure capacity in?* (mL and L)

. Write 235mL + 424mL and **ask:** *Can you work this out using column addition?* Demonstrate the calculation on the whiteboard, drawing attention to the unit of measure at the end of each number and in the answer.

. Write 432g + 264g and ask the pupils to work this out using columns on their own whiteboards. Make sure they check their answers with a partner before checking with you. Make sure all pupils have included the unit of measure in their answers.

. Write 'Peter is a very brave skateboarder. He has a blue and green skateboard that is 27cm long. His friend Gregg has a skateboard that is 15cm longer. What is the length of Gregg's board?' Work through this addition using columns on the board. **Say:** *7 ones add 5 ones equals 1 ten and 2 ones (12), so we need to move the ten underneath and add it on to the tens column. What is the total of the tens column? 2 tens plus 1 ten and add our newly made 1 ten = 4 tens. 27 + 15 = 42cm. Gregg's board is 42cm long.*

. Repeat the use of column addition as you go through more problems that involve length, mass and capacity (e.g. Hamish and William both used the milk this morning. Hamish had 234mL and William had 323mL. How much did they have altogether?).

Key checks: Do the pupils know when to use each measurement? Do the pupils understand the term kilo (kilo = thousand)? Can the pupils use columns to add?

Extension: Allow pupils to work with kg and g and L and mL mixed calculations e.g. 1.2L + 345mL or 1200g + 1.3kg).

Support: Provide pupils with Dienes equipment so that they can physically see the number representation, then encourage pupils to show partitioning understanding as they add numbers. Questions should not cross over the tens barrier.

Subtracting measures

Strand: Measurement

Learning objective: To subtract lengths (m/cm/mm), mass (kg/g) and volume/ capacity (L/mL).

You will need: whiteboards, whiteboard pens, Dienes, number lines, 100 squares

1. Recap the units we use to measure length, mass and capacity.

2. Write 789mL – 345mL on the board and **ask:** *Can you work this out using column subtraction?* Demonstrate the calculation on the whiteboard, drawing attention to the unit of measure at the end of each number and in the answer.

3. Write 1.2kg – 350g and ask the pupils to work this out using columns on their own whiteboards. Make sure all pupils have included the measurement in their answers and have converted kg to g. Remind pupils that 1.2kg is equal to 1200g.

4. Write 'Two bowls of cereal together weigh 543g. One of them weighs 277g. How much does the other weigh?' Work this out with the group using columns on the board:

$$\begin{array}{r} {}^{4\,'3}\!\not{5}\not{4}\,{}^{'}3 \\ -\,2\,7\,7 \\ \hline 2\,6\,6 \end{array}$$

5. **Say:** *7 ones are greater than 3 ones, so 3 ones will have to exchange from 4 tens to make 13. So the calculation becomes 13 takeaway 7.* Move on to the tens column and **Say:** *7 tens are greater than 3 tens, so 3 tens will have to exchange from 5 hundreds to make 13 tens. 13 tens takeaway 7 tens equals 6 tens.* Move on to the hundreds column, **Say:** *4 hundreds takeaway 2 hundreds equals 2 hundreds. So the answer is 266.*

6. Repeat using column subtraction with other measurement problems.

Key checks: Do the pupils know when to use each unit of measure? Do they understand the term kilo (kilo = thousand)? Can pupils use columns to subtract?

Extension: Draw two different sized buckets and label them A and B. Next to bucket A, draw four 1-litre bottles and a 500mL bottle (labelled with amounts). Next to bucket B, draw two 1-litre bottles and one 330mL bottle (labelled with amounts). **Ask:** *How much more water does Bucket A hold than Bucket B?*

Support: Provide pupils with Dienes equipment so that they can physically see the number representation, then encourage pupils to show partitioning understanding as they subtract numbers.

Equivalents

Strand: Measurement

Learning objective: To understand simple equivalence.

You will need: whiteboards, whiteboard pens, rulers, scales, measuring jugs

1. **Ask:** *What do we measure length in? What do we measure mass in? What do we measure capacity in?* **Say:** *Today we are going to investigate equivalent measures.*

2. Give each pupil a ruler. **Ask:** *How many cm are there here?* (e.g. 30cm)

3. **Ask:** *Can you see the smallest marks?* **Say:** *These are called millimetres and there are 10 of these in a centimetre.* **Ask:** *How many centimetres are there in a metre?* (100)

4. **Ask** several questions about mm, cm and m (e.g. *How many millimetres in three centimetres?* (30) *How many centimetres in two metres?* (200)).

5. **Ask:** *How many millilitres are in a litre?* Explain that there are 1000. Tell pupils to fill a measuring jug up to 1000mL (1 litre).

6. Ask several questions about capacity (e.g. *How many millilitres are in three litres?* (3000mL) *How many litres are in 1500mL?* (1.5L)).

7. **Ask:** *How many grams are there in a kilogram?* (1000) Explain that one kilogram is equivalent to 1000 grams.

8. Show the pupils the weighing scales and place objects on them. Weigh an object of one kilogram and **Ask:** *How many grams are there here?* (1000)

9. Repeat with another object and **Ask:** *How many kilograms are there?*

10. Repeat measuring activities and ensure pupils are using the correct vocabulary.

Key checks: Do the pupils know that 'cent' means 100 and that 'kilo' means 1000?

Extension: Pupils use their knowledge of multiplying and dividing by 10 and 100 to convert measures using a written method.

Support: Pupils find objects which are less than one metre long and measure them in centimetres and millimetres. They then find objects that are larger than one metre and measure these in centimetres and metres. Compare one metre, one centimetre and one millimetre. **Ask:** *Which is the largest unit of measurement? Why wouldn't I measure* (large object) *in millimetres?*

Walk around 2-D shapes

Strand: Measurement

Learning objective: To measure the perimeter of simple 2-D shapes.

You will need: whiteboards, whiteboard pens, a variety of 2-D shapes to measure, rulers

1. **Say:** *Today we are going to learn about the perimeter of shapes.*

2. **Ask:** *Does anyone know what perimeter is?* Allow pupils to answer.

3. **Say:** *Perimeter is the distance around a 2-D shape.*

4. Show the pupils a square and **Ask:** *How could we measure the distance around this shape?* Allow pupils to answer.

5. Show pupils how to measure the length of one side of the square using a ruler.

6. Measure to the nearest centimetre.

7. **Ask:** *Do I have to measure all the sides of this shape? Why?* (No, because a square has four equal sides.)

8. **Say:** *We can add the length of all 4 sides together and write down the perimeter or we can multiply by four because all sides measure the same length on a square.* Help pupils work out the perimeter of the square.

9. Repeat with other 2-D shapes.

Key checks: Can pupils give a definition of perimeter with an example? Ensure pupils are using a ruler correctly to measure the shape's side lengths.

Extension: Ask: *If the total perimeter of a square is 24cm, what is the length of one side?* (6cm) *How do you know?*

Support: Provide pupils with thick outlined shapes and a transparent ruler with centimetres only, not millimetres. Concentrate on accurate measuring and recording.

Shopkeeper

Strand: Measurement

Learning objective: To add and subtract amounts of money to give change, using both £ and p in practical contexts.

You will need: whiteboards, whiteboard pens, a variety of objects (which will be priced differently), various coins

- **Ask:** *Who goes shopping? Who spends money? What kind of things do you buy? Do you always give the correct amount? Or do you sometimes get change?*

- **Say:** *Today we will be learning about money and giving change.*

- Show the pupils the objects and give each object a price (from 55p to £5.00).

- **Say:** *Choose two objects you would like to buy and write down what they are.*

- Give the pupils some money (e.g. £7.00) using a range of coins and ask them to work out which coins would be best to use to buy their two objects.

- Pretend to be the shopkeeper and model selling an object and giving the correct change to a pupil (e.g. Pay 75p. Work from 75p using real coins to reach £1. Show thinking on a number line from 75p to £1 in jumps, illustrating the possible coins used).

- Ask that pupil to become the next shopkeeper and to sell something to another pupil. Pupils take turns to be the shopkeeper and give accurate change.

Key checks: Can the pupils identify the various coins? Encourage them to talk through why they give certain change or use certain coins.

Extension: Ask pupils to buy more than two items and to calculate the cost. **Ask:** *What change will you get from £5.00 or £10.00? Can you spend exactly £5.00? What is the least number of coins you can use to pay with?*

Support: Provide pupils with prices ranging from 5p to £1.00. Focus on total amounts and giving change.

How long?

Strand: Measurement

Learning objective: To estimate and read time with increasing accuracy to the nearest minute; record and compare time in terms of seconds, minutes and hours.

You will need: whiteboards, whiteboard pens, stopwatch

1. **Ask:** *How many seconds in a minute? How many minutes in an hour? How many hours in a day?*

2. **Say:** *Today we will be learning about time. We will be estimating the time it takes to do things.* **Ask:** *What is estimating?*

3. **Say:** *Estimating is thinking really hard and finding a solution (educated guess) that is close enough to the right answer.*

4. **Say:** *We are going to see how long it takes you to do things.*

5. **Say:** *Let's estimate how long it will take for (pupil's name) to do 10 star jumps. Do you think it will take just a few seconds or more than a minute? Do you think it will take an hour?* Write suggestions on the board along with the names of the pupils who make the suggestions.

6. Time the activity to see how long it actually takes. Who was the closest/most accurate?

7. Repeat for different activities (saying the alphabet, running around the playground etc.), each time allowing the pupils to time each other using a stopwatch.

8. **Ask:** *How long would it take to walk from here to the city centre? In minutes? In hours? In seconds? What about driving to the city centre? How long would that take?*

9. Repeat this with distances that are relevant to your setting (e.g. the shop, the staffroom, the church).

Key checks: Do the pupils know how many seconds in a minute? Minutes in an hour? Hours in a day? Do they understand what estimating is? Can they use a stopwatch?

Extension: Ask the pupils to calculate the difference in time between the estimated times and the actual times taken to do each activity, reinforcing their understanding that there are 60 seconds in a minute, not 100.

Support: Let the pupils be in control of the stopwatch (with supervision) so that they can see the time to become more aware of the length of time and how long things take. This will also reinforce that there only 60 seconds in a minute, not 100

What time is it?

Strand: Measurement

Learning objective: To read the time to five minutes and the nearest minute on a digital clock and an analogue clock.

You will need: whiteboards, whiteboard pens, analogue clocks for pupils to manipulate

1. **Ask:** *Can you remember how many seconds are in a minute? How many minutes are in an hour?*

2. Draw an analogue clock on the whiteboard and label it like this:

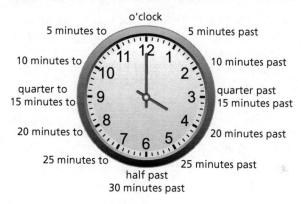

3. **Say:** *An analogue clock face always has two hands: the long hand points to the minutes and the short hand points to the hour.*

4. Work through a few examples of reading the time on an analogue clock. Show a time on an analogue clock and ask pupils to say what time it is.

5. Now say a time and ask pupils to show it on their analogue clocks. **Say:** *Can you show me twenty-five minutes to six?* Repeat for other times.

6. Show a time on an analogue clock and then draw a digital clock on the whiteboard which tells the same time. For example:

7. Repeat with other times. Show the pupils a time on the analogue clock and ask: *Can you write the digital time?*

Key checks: When reading the clock times, are the pupils using '...minutes to' and '...minutes past'? Do they know which hand shows minutes and which hand shows the hours? Can they show an analogue time as a digital time?

Extension: Explain that as there are 24 hours in a day, the time in the morning (a.m.) is 00:00–12:00 and the time in the afternoon/evening (p.m.) is 13:00–24:00. Ask the pupils to draw these 24-hour times on their clocks and to practise writing 24-hour times. If you write the 12-hour time, can they write the corresponding 24-hour time?

Support: Provide pupils with an analogue clock so that they can move the hands to tell the time. Revise reading o'clock, half past, quarter past and quarter to. Do pupils know how many minutes there are per small interval (1) and larger interval (5)? How many minutes in half past, quarter past and quarter to? How many in an hour? Pupils create times for each other exploring five-minute intervals. Link the five-minute intervals to the 5s multiplication table. *Say: If we multiply the number on the clock by five it tells us the number of minutes, for example, 3 × 5 = 15, so when the long hand is on the three it is 15 minutes or quarter past the hour.*

Roman times Bingo

Strand: Measurement

Learning objective: To read Roman numerals from I to XII.

You will need: whiteboards, whiteboard pens, analogue clocks

1. **Say:** *We are going to be learning more about telling the time. Today, we use the numerals 1, 2, 3, 4 and 5, but thousands of years ago the Romans used their own numerals for trading and other things.*

2. Draw the Roman numerals on the board *without* the Arabic equivalent and **ask:** *Has anyone seen these numbers before?* (e.g. on a clock)

1 = I	4 = IV	7 = VII	10 = X
2 = II	5 = V	8 = VIII	11 = XI
3 = III	6 = VI	9 = IX	12 = XII

3. **Say:** *These numerals are still used on some analogue clocks.*

4. Draw a blank clock face on the board (or use a blank clock if you have one).

5. **Ask:** *Can anyone put these numerals in the correct place on a blank clock face?*

6. As a group, write the Roman numerals in the correct place and practise telling the time using them. Display 3 o'clock and **Ask:** *Can you write the time in Roman numerals?* All the pupils should write III. Repeat with several other o'clock times.

7. Play Roman numerals bingo. Pupils split their whiteboards into six sections and choose six Roman numerals. You point the hour hand to a number (e.g. 8 or VIII) and if the pupils have it on their board they cross it out. The winner is the first person to cross out all their numbers and to shout *BINGO!*

Key checks: Can the pupils match the Roman numerals to the digits they see every day (1–12)?

Extension: Pupils convert 24-hour times to Roman numeral and 12-hour times.

Support: Provide pupils with an analogue clock marked with 1–12. Pupils draw Roman numerals on a blank clock and refer to it.

Accurate shapes

Strand: Geometry – properties of shape

Learning objective: To draw 2-D shapes.

You will need: pencils, rulers, paper/exercise book, centimetre-squared paper

1. **Ask:** *What is special about a square?* Allow pupils time to respond.

2. **Say:** *A square has four sides of equal length.*

3. **Ask:** *Can a square have the following measurements: 4cm, 4cm, 5cm, 6cm?* Allow pupils time to digest this and then ask them to try and draw this 'square'.

4. **Ask:** *What is wrong with these measurements?* **Say:** *All the sides must be the same length.*

5. Draw a square that is 4cm, 4cm, 4cm, 4cm. **Ask:** *Is this better?*

6. **Ask:** Can you *draw a rectangle that is 2cm, 4cm, 2cm, 4cm?* Look at their drawings.

7. Discuss where the 2cm sides and the 4cm sides should go. **Ask:** *Why is that important?*

8. Repeat this process with other shapes (hexagon, octagon and triangle) using centimetre-squared paper.

9. **Ask:** Do you *have to use a ruler to measure when drawing on squared paper? Why or why not?* (Using centimetre-squared paper enables the pupils to focus on drawing accurate straight lines.)

Key checks: Do pupils understand that the opposite sides of a rectangle are the same length?

Extension: Introduce pupils to dot paper. Model how to use it to draw accurately. Ask the pupils to create more challenging 2-D shapes (heptagon, nonagon, decagon).

Support: Provide pupils with the 2-D shapes and a centimetre-only ruler. Pupils choose simple shapes and use centimetre-squared paper to draw them.

The angle family

Strand: Geometry – properties of shape

Learning objective: To compare angles with right angles using accurate vocabulary.

You will need: whiteboards, whiteboard pens, protractor

1. **Say:** *Today we will be learning more about angles.*

2. **Ask:** *Does anyone know what a right angle is? Can you show me a right angle? Where can we find them? Can you think of any shapes which have right angles in them? Are there any right angles in this room?*

3. **Ask:** *Does anyone know what unit we use to measure angles?* (degrees)

4. **Ask:** *Does anyone know the names of any other angles?*

5. **Say:** *If an angle is less than 90 degrees we call it an acute angle – an easy way to remember this is that the angle is small and cute like a baby. A-CUTE baby.*

6. Draw several examples of acute angles on the whiteboard and then ask pupils to draw their own.

7. **Say:** *If an angle is bigger than 90 degrees we call it an obtuse angle – so an obtuse angle is larger than a right angle. (Show examples of obtuse angles ranging from 91 and 180 degrees.)*

8. Draw several examples of angles on the whiteboard and ask pupils to copy them. Pupils to label each angle (right, acute and obtuse).

9. Ask the pupils to compare the angles drawn using the symbols <, = and < e.g.

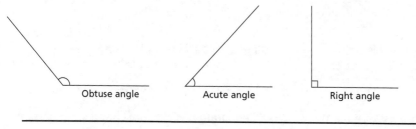

| Obtuse angle | Acute angle | Right angle |

Key checks: Can pupils tell you which angle is bigger or smaller than a right angle? Obtuse or acute angle?

Extension: Ask pupils to draw a shape with: 1 right angle, 2 right angles, 4 right angles, no right angles.

Support: Provide pupils with a transparent 2-D square and model how to use the corner as a true right angle. Ask them to find right angles in objects around the room.

Folding shapes

Strand: Geometry – properties of shape

Learning objective: To identify reflective symmetry in 2-D shapes.

You will need: 2-D shapes on paper (pre-cut out would be beneficial): squares, circles, isosceles and equilateral triangles, rectangles, regular hexagons, regular octagons, pencils and rulers

1. **Say:** *Today we will be learning about symmetry.* **Ask:** *Does anyone know what symmetry is?* **Say:** *Either side of the line of symmetry is a mirror image of the other.*

2. Show the pupils a piece of A4 paper. **Ask:** *What is this shape? Do you think this shape is symmetrical? Is there a way we can test it?*

3. **Say:** *We can fold this shape to see if it is symmetrical. Where could we fold it?*

4. **Say:** *When the folded part sits exactly on top and all the sides/edges are matching, then we call this fold a 'line of symmetry'.* Show an example:

   Say: Here I have folded a rectangle one way, and it **didn't work.**
   So this is **not** a line of symmetry.

   Say: But when I try it this way, it **does work** (the folded part sits perfectly on top, all edges matching). So this **is** a line of symmetry.

5. Repeat this process with the other shapes with pupils doing the folding. Discuss where the lines of symmetry are and draw them on the shapes using a ruler.

Key checks: Are the pupils folding accurately? Some will need support. Can the pupils point to where the line of symmetry will be before they fold the shape?

Extension: Pupils find lines of symmetry in more difficult 2-D shapes (heptagon, nonagon and decagon). Display shapes at a different angle and ask if they still have symmetry (e.g. a regular square stood slightly on one vertex).

Support: Provide pupils with the 2-D paper shapes, first squares and rectangles. Follow with equilateral triangles and circles. Pupils can fold the paper shapes and see what happens when a shape does and does not have symmetry.

Different lines

Strand: Geometry – properties of shape

Learning objective: To identify horizontal, vertical, perpendicular and parallel lines.

You will need: whiteboards, whiteboard pens

1. **Say:** *Today we will be looking at different types of lines.*

2. Draw a horizontal line and **Ask:** *What kind of line is this?* **Say:** *A line drawn from left to right or right to left is called horizontal. This word is similar to 'horizon', which is the line where the land meets the sky.*

3. Draw a vertical line and **Ask:** *What kind of line is this?* **Say:** *A line drawn from bottom to top or top to bottom is called vertical. The word vertical comes from the word 'vertigo', which is a fear of being up high.*

4. Draw vertical and horizontal lines on the board and ask the pupils to name them.

5. Ask the pupils to draw and label horizontal and vertical lines.

6. Draw perpendicular lines on the board and **Say:** *When two lines are at right angles to each other they are perpendicular.*

7. Ask the pupils to draw examples of perpendicular lines. **Ask:** *Can you find any perpendicular lines in the classroom? Or think of any outside the classroom?*

8. Draw parallel lines on the board and **Say:** *When two lines are always the same distance apart and never touch, like a train track or how the two ls in the word parallel are next to each other.*

9. Ask the pupils to draw examples of parallel lines. **Ask:** *Can you find any parallel lines in the classroom? Or think of any outside the classroom?*

Key checks: Can the pupils give an example of a horizontal, vertical, perpendicular and parallel line somewhere in the classroom? (e.g. vertical blinds, horizontal window, perpendicular lines of the door, parallel edge of the table top).

Extension: Challenge pupils to draw and identify quadrilaterals; with perpendicular and parallel lines (square, rectangle); with only parallel lines, no perpendicular lines (trapezium, rhombus, parallelogram); with only perpendicular lines, no parallel lines (irregular quadrilateral).

Support: Give pupils horizontal and vertical labels. Pupils find horizontal and vertical lines in the classroom and stick labels on. Ask the pupils to discuss and explain their choices. Can pupils label horizontal and vertical lines in different shapes?

Shape animals

Strand: Geometry – properties of shape

Learning objective: To make 3-D shapes using modelling materials.

You will need: a wide variety of 3-D shape nets (cubes, cuboids, spheres, different prisms, different pyramids), scissors, colouring pens/pencils, a large quantity of straws, blu-tack, a feely bag with shapes in it

1. **Say:** *Today you will be creating your very own shape animals.*

2. Show the pupils a cuboid and **Ask:** *What shape is this? What are the properties of this shape?* Steer the discussion towards faces, vertices and edges. Make sure pupils understand each of these words.

3. **Say:** *A cube has six square faces, eight vertices and 12 edges.*

4. Show the pupils the straws and blu-tack.

5. **Say:** *Today we are going to use the straws and blu-tack to make our own 3-D shapes.*

6. Model making a cube using the equipment. Once made, reiterate the properties of the cube whilst pointing to them. Provide the pupils with time to create their own 3-D shapes.

7. **Say:** *We will use 3-D shapes to try and create our own shape animal.*

8. Allow the pupils to choose a 3-D shape(s).

9. Once the pupils have created their shape, with long/short straws and blu-tack they can use it to design an animal around the skeleton frame.

Key checks: Can pupils describe the properties of the shapes (edges, vertices and faces)?

Extension: Ask the pupils to use a feely bag and then ask them to feel for the cube, cuboid or other 3-D shapes. Ask them how they know they have the right shape without removing it from the bag. Can they describe the shape to the rest of the group?

Support: Give pupils 3-D shapes to see and feel. **Ask:** *What 2-D shapes can you see on the surface of this shape? What do we call them on 3-D shapes?* (faces) Pupils use 2-D shapes to create the net of the 3-D shape and draw around them. They cut out and fold the shape together. **Ask:** *What properties can you see?*

Turning around

Strand: Geometry – properties of shape

Learning objective: To recognise that two right angles make a half-turn, three make three-quarters of a turn and four a complete turn.

You will need: whiteboards, whiteboard pens

1. **Ask:** *Do you know what the points of a compass are?* (North, East, South, West)

2. **Ask:** *How do you or how can you remember them?* (Never Eat Shredded Wheat/Naughty Elephants Squirt Water, etc.)

3. **Say:** *Each compass point is a right angle turn from the one before and the one after.*

4. **Ask:** *Do you know which way is clockwise and which way is anticlockwise?*

5. Draw a compass rose on the whiteboard.

6. **Ask:** *If we face north and turn a quarter turn, where will we face?* (east) **Say:** *Stand facing north and take two turns clockwise or a half-turn. Which way are you now facing?* (south)

7. Repeat with different directions both clockwise and anticlockwise.

Key checks: If they are facing north, do pupils know how many quarter turns they need to face south? Do they know if they are moving clockwise or anti-clockwise? Do they know how many quarter turns makes a complete turn?

Extension: Pupils use whole, quarter, three-quarters and half-turns using shapes/objects on a grid. Pupils explain how the object moves across the grid.

Support: Focus on quarter turns and making connections with right angles. Have a large compass displayed on the floor with the points labelled N, E, S, W and $\frac{1}{4}$ written at each interval. Discuss how $\frac{1}{4}$ then $\frac{1}{2}$ then $\frac{3}{4}$ then a complete turn occurs. Work through many examples.

Tally up

Strand: Statistics

Learning objective: To present data.

You will need: whiteboards, whiteboard pens, counters, different coloured pencils/pens

1. **Ask:** *Do you know what data means?* **Say:** *It means information.*

2. **Ask:** *How do people collect data?* **Say:** *Data is often collected by asking a question. For example, 'Do you prefer oranges or apples?'*

3. **Say:** *People create surveys to find out what people like or think or what people have done.*

4. Draw the following on the whiteboard:

Fruit	Tally	Number
Apples	J̶H̶T̶ III	8
Oranges	J̶H̶T̶ J̶H̶T̶ II	12

5. **Say:** *This is a tally chart. Tally charts help us collect data and keep track of our counting.*

6. **Ask:** *How could we represent this information using pictures?*

7. **Say:** *We could use a pictogram to show it. A pictogram is a visual representation of data that has been collected, like this:*

Fruit	
Apples	🍎🍎🍎🍎🍎🍎🍎🍎
Oranges	🍊🍊🍊🍊🍊🍊🍊🍊🍊🍊🍊🍊

8. **Say:** *Each picture in a pictogram represents one or more objects or actions. For example, each* ▨ *in this pictogram represents two books.* **Ask:** *How many books did each person read?*

Name	Books read
Ayumi	▨ ▨
Anna	▨ ▨ ▨ ▨
Alan	▨ ▨ ▨
Steve	▨ ▨

9. As a group, draw the tally chart to match this pictogram. **Say:** *Can you help me to draw the tally chart for this data?*

10. Ask pupils to think of a question to find out the group's favourite sweets and create a tally chart. Ask the pupils to use different colours to represent the same data in a pictogram.

Key checks: Can pupils answer questions about a pictogram and show understanding of what one symbol represents? Can they interpret both vertical and horizontal picture graphs?

Extension: Challenge the pupils, **Ask:** *Can you represent your tally chart using a block graph? What does your data tell you?*

Support: Practise tallying different numbers so that pupils explore tallying five and above. When pupils create a question, limit the number of people they ask to 10 to enable them to record the data easily.

Survey says...

Strand: Statistics

Learning objective: To find answers to questions, collect data and analyse.

You will need: whiteboards, whiteboard pens, paper, pens/pencils

1. **Say:** *Today we are going to collect and display data.* **Ask:** *Can you remember how people collect data?*

2. **Say:** *People often use surveys to find out what people like or have done.*

3. **Ask:** *What is the group's favourite colour?*

4. Create a tally chart together, e.g.

Colour	Tally	Number
Blue	JHT	5
Pink	I I	2

5. **Ask:** *How could we show this information for people to read easily?* **Say:** *We could draw a pictogram.* Draw a pictogram together, e.g.

Blue	● ● ● ● ●
Pink	○ ○

6. **Ask:** *What does our pictogram tell us? How many people liked the colour blue?*

7. As a group, decide on a question to ask other pupils and then take a survey, fill in a tally chart and create a pictogram.

Key checks: Can the pupils link the visual representation of the tally and the pictogram?

Extension: Pupils collect data and present results with a key that shows one symbol representing two items (e.g. two cats or dogs). Pupils explain their findings. **Ask:** *What do you notice? Did anything surprise you? Which was the most / least popular? What was the difference between the least and most popular (range)?*

Support: Give pupils a tally. Can they use the information to create a pictogram with a title? Can they explain something that their data tells you?

IMPACT
Intervention
English Activities

Proper prefixes

Strand: Reading – word reading

Learning objective: To apply their growing knowledge of root words and prefixes, both to read aloud and to understand the meaning of new words they meet.

You will need: whiteboards, whiteboard pens and rubbers, dictionaries, flashcards with prefixes un–,dis–, mis–, ir–, in–, im–, il–, sub– and super–

1. **Ask:** *What is a prefix?* (a group of letters that join onto the front of a word and change the meaning of the root word)

2. **Ask:** *Can you give me any examples of words with the prefix un–?* (e.g. undo, unkind) **Say:** *Dis– and mis– are like un– – they also change the meaning of the word to the opposite. For example, appear – disappear, understand – misunderstand.* **Ask:** *Can you think of other examples? Write them down. Can you underline the root word? Can you circle the prefix?*

3. **Say:** *Look at the words with prefixes. Do they have positive or negative meanings?* Establish that these prefixes give a negative meaning.

4. Check for misconceptions. Write the word 'university' on the whiteboard and **Ask:** *Does this word contain a prefix?* **Say:** *If you remove the un, it leaves 'iversity' which isn't a root word.* Repeat for 'disaster' and 'misery'. **Say:** *To be a prefix, the letters must change the meaning of a root word.*

5. Write the prefixes in–, im–, il– and ir– on the whiteboard. **Say:** *We are going to work out when to use each of these prefixes. Use a dictionary to find two words starting with each prefix (in–, im–, il– and ir–) and write them on your whiteboard. Check that you have a root word if you remove the prefix letters.*

6. Discuss what the rules might be with reference to the words they have found. **Say:** *The spelling rules are: If the root word starts with l, use il– (illegal). If the root word starts with m or p use im– (impossible, immature). If the root word starts with r, use ir– (irregular). All other times, use in– (insane, insecure).*

7. Write the prefixes sub– and super– on the whiteboard. **Say:** *Can you work out the meanings of these prefixes by looking at some examples?* Write submarine, subheading, subway, superstar, superhuman, supercharged. **Say:** *Sub– means under. Super– means above. Now use a dictionary to look up some more words with the prefixes sub– and super–.*

8. Show flashcards with the prefixes anti–, auto–, inter– and re–. On the other side will be the meaning of each prefix: anti– = against, auto– = self, inter– = between, re– = again/back. **Say:** *Here are even more prefixes. Can you*

work out their meaning by looking up words in the dictionary? For example, antifreeze, antigravity, automatic, autobiography, autograph, intercity, interact, international, redo, refresh, redecorate.

Key checks: Do pupils understand what a prefix is? Do they understand that the prefix letters change the meaning of the root word? Do they understand that some words starting with prefix letters are not words containing prefixes (e.g. insect, instruct, subject).

Extension: Ask pupils to use the words in sentences or to find examples of words and prefixes in their reading. Provide flashcards with words that contain prefixes and words that don't (misconception words) and ask pupils to identify which ones do. **Ask:** *Can you write some more words that begin with un– / dis– / mis– / in– / im– / il– / ir– / sub– / super– where these letters are not prefixes?*

Support: Split the session so two or three prefixes are covered each time. Allow pupils time to use each prefix. Provide root words and a choice of prefixes to match using a dictionary.

Supplementary suffixes

Strand: Reading – word reading

Learning objective: To apply their growing knowledge of root words and suffixes both to read aloud and to understand the meaning of new words they meet.

You will need: whiteboards, whiteboard pens and rubbers, access to reading books

1. **Ask:** *What is a suffix?* (a group of letters that are added to the end of words)
   Ask: *Does a suffix change the meaning of the root word?* (yes)

2. **Say:** *Let's work out the spelling rule for adding the suffix –ation.* Write information, preparation and adoration on the whiteboard. **Ask:** *Can you work out the root words?*

3. **Ask:** *Can you work out how the suffix –ation is added?* (Straight on to a verb to form a noun, e.g. inform + ation = information. If the root word ends in 'e', drop the 'e', e.g. prepar(–e) + ation = preparation.)

4. **Say:** *Now let's work out the spelling rule for the suffix –ly.* Write sadly on the whiteboard. **Ask:** *Can you work out the root word? Can you spot the spelling rule? The suffix –ly starts with a consonant, so is directly added to most adjectives to form an adverb: sad – sadly.* **Ask:** *Can you think of any other words with the suffix –ly?* (e.g. finally, completely, kindly) **Say:** *But if the root word ends with 'y', you need to change the 'y' to 'i' and then add –ly: happy – happily.* **Ask:** *Can you think of any other words that follow this rule?* (e.g. angrily)

5. Write 'gentle' and 'simple' on the board. **Ask:** *How do we add the suffix –ly to words which end in 'le'?* (change the –le to –ly)

6. **Say:** *Now let's look at the suffix –ous.* Write poisonous, mountainous and famous on the whiteboard. For each one, **Ask:** *Can you work out the root word? Now can you spot the spelling rule?* (The usual spelling rules for adding suffixes that start with a vowel letter apply. See step 2.)

Key checks: Does each pupil understand what a suffix is? Can each pupil identify the root word? Can each pupil explain how to add the suffix?

Extension: Can pupils explain how adding a suffix has changed the word class? For example, the adjective 'grand' has become an adverb 'grandly' by adding the suffix –ly. Ask pupils to find examples of words and their suffixes in their reading books and write these on a whiteboard.

Support: Split the session so two suffixes are covered each time. Allow pupils time to practise using the suffix. Provide root words and a choice of suffixes to match using a dictionary.

Say it to spell it

Strand: Reading – word reading

Learning objective: To read further exception words, noting the unusual correspondences between spelling and sound.

You will need: whiteboards, whiteboard pens and rubbers

Say: *We are going to learn to spell some tricky words. These words have letters that don't follow usual spelling rules. They are exceptions. We can call them exception words.* Discuss what 'exception' means using understanding of the root word 'except'.

Write 'favourite' on the whiteboard. **Ask:** *Where is the tricky part of the word?* (our) Underline this part of the word. **Say:** *I know we say fave-rit, but to help us spell the word correctly let's say it as it is spelt: fav-our-i-te.* Write the word at the same time as saying it. **Say:** *Now it's your turn.* Pupils should say *fav-our-i-te* and write the word correctly on their whiteboards. Finish by saying the word correctly together.

Say: *What about the word centre? Is that a tricky word to spell? Can anyone spell centre? I know we say 'senter', but to help us spell the word correctly let's say ken-tre.* Write the word (correctly) at the same time as saying it. **Say:** *Now it's your turn.* Pupils should say *ken-tre* and write the word correctly on their whiteboards. Finish by saying the word correctly together.

Say: *What about the word island? Is that a tricky word to spell? Can anyone here spell island? I know we say 'eyeland', but to help us spell the word correctly let's say iz-land.* Write the word at the same time as saying it. **Say:** *Now it's your turn.* Pupils should say *iz-land* and write the word correctly on their whiteboards. Finish by saying the word correctly together.

Say: *What about the word special? Is that a tricky word to spell? Can anyone here spell special? I know we say 'speshul', but to help us spell the word correctly let's say spek-ee-al.* Write the word at the same time as saying it. **Say:** *Now it's your turn.* Pupils should say *spek-ee-al* and write the word correctly on their whiteboards. Finish by saying the word correctly together.

Key checks: Are pupils saying the word as it is spelt to support spelling? Can pupils recognise the written word and read it correctly?

Extension: Dictate a short sentence to include the tricky word. **Say:** *My favourite game is Minecraft.*

Support: Practise the word in many ways, including 'look, cover, write, check', rainbow writing, pyramid writing, or mnemonics.

I love reading

Strand: Reading – comprehension

Learning objective: To participate in discussion about both books that are read to them and those they can read for themselves, taking turns and listening to what others say.

Note: This will need to be done throughout the year using different genres of books. It could be covered during group guided reading sessions.

You will need: a range of books

1. **Questions to ask for fiction:** • *Who is telling the story?* • *What are the main conflicts/problems and how are they resolved?* • *Were there parts of the story you didn't understand?* • *How was the setting important?* • *What mood/ atmosphere did it create?* • *Have you read any other similar stories? Seen similar plots or characters?*

2. **Questions to ask for poetry:** • *How do you feel when you read the poem?* • *What picture does the poet create in your mind?* • *Tell me about the structure/pattern of the poem.* • *Do you prefer this poem or...?* • *Which phrase or phrases in the poem do you think describe the subject of the poem the most successfully?* (particularly simile/metaphor) • *Are there any words you are not sure about?*

3. **Questions to ask for non-fiction:** • *What kinds of things interest you about this book?* • *What questions do you think the book would be able to answer?* • *Where would you find the definition of a word you don't understand?* • *How does the layout of the book support its purpose?* • *Do you think the book is presented in an interesting way?* • *What have you learned from the pages you've just read?* • *Can you write a true or false question about what you've just read?* • *What research do you think the author needed to do before writing the book?*

Key checks: Are pupils able to take part in discussion? Do pupils have strategies to use if they do not fully understand new vocabulary?

Extension: Ask pupils to prove their answers by finding examples within the text.

Support: Point pupils to a particular page or paragraph for them to find evidence to support their answer.

A reading puzzle

Strand: Reading – comprehension

Learning objective: To develop positive attitudes to reading and understanding of what they read by reading books that are structured in different ways and reading for a range of purposes.

You will need: a variety of books, leaflets, newspapers, magazines, letters, notes, emails, whiteboard, whiteboard pen and rubber

1. **Say:** *We are going to solve a reading puzzle today.* **Ask:** *Why do we need to be able to read?* Discuss. **Say:** *There are so many things we need and want to read, aren't there? For example, visiting a museum or looking at information on the computer, completing forms or shopping online all involve reading. Split the pupils into pairs. Can you tell your partner one more thing that requires reading?*

2. Give each pupil two contrasting books or leaflets (e.g. a picture book and an information book) and ask them to hunt for different features. **Ask:** *Does either text contain an index? Are there subheadings? Can you find chapters?* Other features to look for: photographs, labels, captions, diagrams, paragraphs, tables, fact boxes, contents, glossary.

3. Ask questions about the reason for the writing. **Ask:** *Who has this been written for? What is the reason for writing it? Why might you read it?*

4. Repeat with other examples of different types of reading material to focus pupils on the structure and purpose of each one. Focus on how they are the same and how they are different.

Key checks: Do pupils understand the purpose/reason of the text? Do they understand how a story created for a child is different from one for teenagers? e.g. teenage text has fewer pictures, is arranged in chapters, has smaller text, longer words, longer sentences)

Extension: Say: *Make a list of the features you find in each type of reading material.* For example, a picture book: paragraphs, pictures, title; a non-fiction book: photographs, labels, captions, diagrams, paragraphs, subheadings, tables, fact boxes, index, contents, glossary.

Support: Provide a choice of responses, and encourage pupils to repeat responses so they get used to using the language. For example: **Ask:** *Who has it been written for?* **Structured response:** *A child because it uses simple words or an adult because the words are longer and trickier.* **Ask:** *What is the reason for writing it?* **Structured response:** *It is a story for enjoyment or a book with instructions.*

Dictionary detectives

Strand: Reading – comprehension

Learning objective: To use a dictionary to check the meaning of words that they have read.

You will need: a set of books, for example, guided reading books, dictionary (if you are looking up specific vocabulary, ensure you use a dictionary that contains the words)

1. **Say:** *Today you are going to look at a story book with some words you are not familiar with.* **Ask:** *When you read a word you are not sure about, what could you do to be sure about its meaning?* (use a dictionary) **Say:** *A dictionary uses alphabetical order to help us find words quickly. Does everybody know their alphabet?* Pupils recite the alphabet.

2. Choose a book with a difficult word in the title or a chapter heading, for example, a book about the prehistoric era. **Ask:** *What does 'era' mean?*

3. **Say:** *How do I use a dictionary to find 'era'?* Walk pupils through how to use their knowledge of alphabetical order to find the word. **Say:** *We are going to skim and scan to find 'era'. First, skim to find the letter 'e'. We know that 'e' is quite early in the alphabet so it will be near the front of the dictionary. Here are some 'e' words. The next letter in the word is 'r', so now I am looking for 'er'. 'r' is close to the end of the alphabet so I can skim past these words until I find words with 'er'. 'a' is the first letter of the alphabet so now I need to scan the words more slowly until I find 'era'. The dictionary says an 'era' is 'A period of time marked by distinctive events'. So the prehistoric era is a period of time marked by the stone age, iron age and bronze age. What does 'distinctive' mean? What can we do if we don't know the meaning of a word in the dictionary? Use your dictionary to find the definition. See if you can find the definition of distinctive. Go!*

4. Once pupils are confident with the process, get them to look up three or four further words.

Key checks: Are pupils confident with alphabetical order? This is particularly important for pupils with English as an additional language. Can pupils identify the theme of the book?

Extension: Provide a word list of topic-related vocabulary for pupils to look up and define.

Support: Use a simpler dictionary or the glossary at the back of a book, but ensure it contains specific words if you are looking at a particular book.

Tell me a story

Strand: Reading – comprehension

Learning objective: To increase their familiarity with a wide range of books, including fairy stories, myths and legends and retelling some of these orally.

You will need: a fairy story, myth or legend, a 'new words list' (look through the chosen story in advance), paper, pencils/coloured pencils/pens

1. **Say:** *In order to be able to tell someone a story, it's easiest to think about a story you know well. You can make it exciting to listen to. This is called re-telling, and we are going to learn to do this.*

2. Select a story the pupils are not familiar with. **Say:** *Old stories, such as fairy tales, myths and legends often have different versions written down. It is possible you will have heard a similar story before.*

3. Tell the pupils briefly about the story – introduce the main characters, setting and plot. Also introduce any new vocabulary you think they will find particularly tricky and display this on a 'new word list'.

4. **Ask:** *Can you read the story yourself?* When the group has read half the story, you take over the reading, so they can hear how sentences should sound, where to pause and so on.

5. The pupils will need to re-read the story a few times to become familiar with it. Prepare for re-telling by writing a particular word or phrase you want pupils to include from that part of the story (for example, deep, dark forest; hairy, scary wolf). **Say:** *Read the story phrases we are going to include.*

6. **Say:** *We are going to use the story phrases to re-tell the story. We need to include enough information for someone who hasn't read the story to understand what it is about. We also need to make it sound exciting.* **Ask:** *How can we do this?* Allow time for pupils to think and take feedback. **Say:** *We can vary our voices to make it sound exciting for someone listening.* Model an example *Once upon a time, there lived a little old lady in the middle of a deep, dark forest. Also in the wood lived a hairy, scary wolf.*

Key checks: Can pupils recognise and read the new vocabulary within the story? Can pupils remember the events in order? Is the re-telling engaging for a listener?

Extension: Ask pupils to listen to each other re-telling the story. Is their partner remembering to use all the listed words and phrases? Are they interesting to listen to?

Support: Have pupils each draw a picture of a certain character, setting, thing or event that the group agree are important in the story, and then place these in order to help pupils remember the phrases.

Book themes

Strand: Reading – comprehension

Learning objective: To identify the themes and conventions in a wide range of books.

Note: You will need to assess this objective using some of the following questions. It will need to be revisited a few times during the year, in order to achieve the 'wide range' part of the learning objective.

You will need: a collection of less well-known fairy stories, myths and legends (e.g. the story of Icarus), prepare a 'new words list', theme flashcards

1. Introduce a book pupils do not know well. **Say:** *We are going to talk about this story, and think about other stories that are similar that you already know.*

2. Read the story, myth or legend. It should be closely matched to the pupils' ability.

3. **Ask a range of questions, for example:**

   - *Is the main character like someone you know?*

   - *This story is a myth. What phrases show it is a myth?*

   - *Is this story set now or in the past? How do you know?*

   - *What is the moral of the story?*

   - *What do we learn from the story?*

   - *Do you know any other stories like this? What happens in them? How are they similar? How are they different?*

   _____

Key checks: Can pupils read the story fluently? Do they require an easier text?

Extension: Give pupils a second version of the same story, and **Say:** *Let's compare the two versions. Are the same details included? Which book do you think would be more suitable for a younger child and why?*

Support: Provide examples of themes from the story on flashcards. For example pets, friendship, changes, the weather, learning from our mistakes, etc. **Ask:** *Which theme is the story about? How do you know?*

Perfect performance – Vary your voice

trand: Reading – comprehension

earning objective: To prepare poems and play scripts to read aloud and perform.

ou will need: a poem and a play script appropriate for Year 3 pupils, copies for upils to annotate, coloured pencils

ote: This activity could be split across two sessions.

First, read the selected poem. **Say:** *Notice how the poem is arranged on the page. Where should you pause? How will you vary your voice? Which parts will be louder, which will be quieter?*

Ask: *Will you vary the pace of each line? Do some parts of the poem seem to race along? You could read these words more quickly.*

Allow pupils time to practise reading the poem aloud to themselves. **Say:** *Now, you are going to perform your poem for your partner. Partners should listen carefully and say what they enjoyed about the performance, for example, by giving two stars and a wish.* Swap roles.

Show pupils the play script and assign roles. **Say:** *We are going to act out a play today. You will need to vary your voice in order to be a convincing actor.*

Support pupils to prepare their role. **Ask:** *Is your character in every scene? Are you able to read all the words? Can you underline the words you say? Are there any stage directions? (words you act, but do not say) Do you know how your character is feeling? Can you use your voice to show that?*

Encourage pupils to follow each other's lines so they say their character's words at the appropriate time.

---

ey checks: Are pupils able to vary their voices to show the mood of the poem the mood of their character? Are they able to follow stage directions?

xtension: Pupils could perform to a larger audience. For example, a playtime erformance or talent show-type assembly.

upport: Pupils use coloured pencils to annotate the poem/play script to help ompt pace, volume and actions. Pupils may need feedback, for example, two ars and a wish modelled for them. For example, **Say:** *Do you like the way ame) is changing her voice in this line, or in this line better?*

Lovely language

Strand: Reading – comprehension

Learning objective: To discuss words and phrases that capture the reader's imagination.

You will need: copies of 'Anansi the spider' or 'Anansi and the impossible quest' (an Ashanti tale), a whiteboard and pen

1. **Say:** *I am going to read a story about Anansi the spider. This is a tale told by the Ashanti people in West Africa. Follow the story in your copy of the book. Every time we read a word and you don't know what it means, I want you to say 'stop'.*

2. Start to read the story. **Ask:** *Which word is new?* Praise pupils for stopping to clarify the meaning of a word. **Say:** *I am really pleased you asked because that is a tricky word.*

3. Write words on a whiteboard that indicate another culture, for example, descriptions of food, setting, clothing.

4. **Say:** *What does this word mean? What makes you think that?* Having discussed the meaning of the new words, re-read the story without interruption. Find examples of the clothing and food, real if possible, otherwise images from the Internet.

5. During the second read, discuss phrases within the story that are particularly successful. **Ask:** *Which phrase do you particularly like? Which words make you think the story is set in Africa?*

6. Ask questions about the plot or characters, and encourage pupils to use the new vocabulary in their answers. **Ask:** *Why were there 47 stinging hornets in the story? What did the Sky God control?*

Key checks: Are pupils able to select words or phrases that capture the imagination? These may be phrases that describe the different culture in the story.

Extension: Read a folktale from another part of the world and look for words and phrases that capture the reader's imagination, for example, a vivid description of the setting.

Support: Offer pupils phrases from the story to discuss. **Say:** *Which of these phrases do you really like? Can you say what you like about it?*

Poetry patterns

Strand: Reading – comprehension

Learning objective: To recognise some different forms of poetry: free verse and narrative poetry.

You will need: a copy of 'The Owl and The Pussycat' by Edward Lear, examples of narrative and free verse poems, definitions of language features (simile, alliteration, onomatopoeia), highlighter pens. Prepare the poems (one free verse and one narrative) by cutting one stanza of each poem into lines.

1. **Say:** *Here are two cut-up poems. See if you can put the lines of the poem in order.* Give pairs of pupils the cut-up poems and allow time to put both poems in order. **Ask:** *Which poem was easier to order? Why?*

2. **Ask:** *Can you explain how the two poems are different?* Allow pupils time to think, and take their feedback. **Say:** *Free verse has no set structure or pattern, while a narrative poem tells a story and often has more rhyming words. The writer can choose their own pattern in free verse poetry. Free verse poetry can also be narrative.*

3. Read some examples of free verse poetry **Ask:** *Can you choose five words that you felt were the most important in the poem? Why did you select these words?*

4. **Ask:** *Can you highlight all the adjectives in one colour and the similes in another? Is there more of one type of word? What do you think the effect is?*

5. Read 'The Owl and the Pussycat'. **Ask:** *How is this different to free verse?* **Say:** *This is narrative poetry, because it tells a story. It is not like free verse poetry because there is a set rhythmical pattern.* Make sure the pupils understand all the vocabulary.

6. **Ask:** *What is the same and what is different about the two types of poetry? Do you have a preference?* **Say:** *Your opinion is what you think, it cannot be right or wrong, as long as you give a reason.* Ask pupils to use the sentence starter: *"I prefer this poem… because…"*

Key checks: Are pupils able to distinguish between the different forms of poetry?

Extension: Pupils autonomously look up the tricky vocabulary using a dictionary. Pupils write their own free verse and narrative poem. **Ask:** *Which was easier to write? Why?*

Support: Make sure the poems have words pupils are able to access. Read only verse one of 'The Owl and the Pussycat'. Support pupils to give opinions.

Active reading

Strand: Reading – comprehension

Learning objective: To read with understanding, checking that the text makes sense to them.

You will need: a set of books/poems (e.g. guided reading books), prepared questions about the book (there are often prepared questions for guided reading books, or use questions from the 'I love reading' activity), prepared sentence to be displayed: 'Polite notice, please keep off the grass.'

1. **Say:** *I have noticed your reading is becoming more confident, but beware of making mistakes when rushing.* Read the sentence *'Polite notice, please keep off the grass.'* as *'Police notice, please keep off the grass.'*

2. **Ask:** *What was the mistaken word? What happened to the meaning of the sentence?*

3. Discuss words that are commonly misread, e.g. through/though, surprise/suppose, learn/lean. **Ask:** *How can you make sure you are not reading the wrong word?*

4. Talk about active listening as they read. Model this using the book. Read aloud more slowly and model the thought processes out loud. **Say:** *Does that sound right? Do I understand what I'm reading? This is self-checking.* After reading a sentence or paragraph, stop and reiterate the main ideas, e.g. **Say:** *So, these characters are brother and sister and they're on holiday.* Ideally, there will be an unfamiliar word that you will need to think about; stop and discuss this with the group.

5. After you have modelled reading through a page, **Say:** *Now it's your turn to read the book, and I would like you to use a similar self-checking process.*

6. Question the pupils to check their understanding. **Ask:** *Were there any words you were unsure of? What happened to the characters when…?*

Key checks: Are pupils reading slowly and carefully? Can pupils answer questions about what they have read?

Extension: Pupils write their responses to the questions from step 6. Pupils to have a book with less familiar language or extra similes and metaphors. Pupils create a poster of strategies to help when reading.

Support: Have words that pupils are likely to misread written on flashcards and displayed throughout the activity. You could place a flashcard over a similar word in the text and re-read the sentence discussing how it changes the meaning.

Get to know the characters

Strand: Reading – comprehension

Learning objective: To ask and answer questions to improve their understanding of a text.

You will need: a set of books carefully matched to the pupils' reading ability, for example, guided reading books, a spinner with character names as the outcomes (optional)

Note: This session should follow the reading of a familiar story.

1. **Say:** *Think about the book we have just read.* **Ask:** *What would you like to know more about?*

2. If pupils find it difficult to answer this question, you could spin a spinner and ask them to think of a question about the character the spinner points to. This will provide more structure. **Say:** *Can you think of a question about this character? What else would you like to know?*

3. Pupils may want to know everyday things about characters. If pupils are getting stuck, you could suggest questions such as: *What is their favourite food? What do they play with? What is their favourite colour? Do they have a pet?* Encourage the group to look through the text and see if there is any evidence to support an answer, or if we simply do not know. **Say:** *What clues can you find in the book to prove you're right?*

4. Make sure each pupil asks a question. **Ask:** *Do we know the characters better now? Does this change our understanding about the story? Does this change how we feel about the story?*

Key checks: Can each pupil formulate a question?

Extension: Pupils write the questions and responses. They could write a character description before and after the deeper questioning. Confident pupils to be hot-seated as a chosen character to answer questions.

Support: Model asking the question before expecting pupils to do this. Have sentence starters or question stems ready to support pupils.

Find the evidence

Strand: Reading – comprehension

Learning objective: To draw inferences such as inferring characters' feelings, thoughts and motives from their actions, and justifying inferences with evidence.

You will need: a set of books carefully matched to the pupils' reading ability, for example, guided reading books

Notes: This session should follow the reading of a familiar story. Inferential questions are sometimes referred to as 'hidden' questions, the evidence is in the text, however it is not instantly obvious. For example, it would be inferred that a character was unpleasant or mean if the story suggested they were always grumpy, or grimacing. The character's speech could also infer unpleasantness, for example *"Good morning" she said with a false smile.* The character's actions could also infer unpleasantness. For example, *"She opened the door and squinted unkindly at the child standing on the doorstep."*

Ask:

- *Which words make you think this character is unpleasant/mean?*

- *Which words make you like/dislike this character? Why has the author chosen those words?*

- *Which character is funny? How has the author used adjectives to create that character?*

Note: Vary the questions according to the session or book.

Key checks: Can pupils use the text (individual words or phrases) to support them to find answers to their questions?

Extension: Ask the pupils to write their responses.

Support: Ask fewer questions and support pupils with the section of the book where they will find the evidence.

What happens next?

Strand: Reading – comprehension

Learning objective: To predict what might happen from details stated and implied.

You will need: whiteboards, whiteboard pens and rubbers, a set of books (e.g. guided reading books) – a mystery story is particularly good

Note: This session should follow the reading of the first part of a story.

1. **Say:** *Part of understanding a story is to make a prediction about what could happen. A mystery story is full of twists and turns to make the reader think one thing, while the characters do something else. Characters can change how they act, which can change what you think will happen next. Usually one character or group of characters is trying to follow clues to solve the mystery.* **Ask:** *Can you think of any mystery stories?*

2. Make sure the group has read the first part of the story; if necessary, recap the main events.

3. **Ask:** *What is the problem in the story?* • *Who are the characters?* • *Is there a guilty character? How has the author made you think that? What do you think this character will do next? Why? How do you think the other characters will respond?* • *Has the author included any details that seem odd or out of place? How do you think these may be important later?*

4. Continue reading the story. Repeat the questions as pupils read or when you want to draw attention to the fact that new information has been given. It could be useful to keep track of who the suspects are and why, either on a whiteboard or in the pupils' books.

5. At the end of the story **Ask:** *Was your prediction right? Which clues made you think it was this suspect?* Review the notes that were made during the story.

Key checks: Are pupils able to make predictions? If they are incorrect, the author has done a good job of misleading their thinking in the story.

Extension: Pupils may read on independently, making notes when they change their mind about the perpetrator of the crime or the outcome of the mystery.

Support: Make notes on a whiteboard to support pupils through different points in the story. Ask fewer questions and help pupils find the section of the book where they will find the evidence.

In a nutshell

Strand: Reading – comprehension

Learning objective: To be able to identify and summarise the main ideas.

You will need: a set of books (e.g. guided reading books or an article from a newspaper or printed from a website)

1. **Say:** *Have you heard the phrase, 'In a nutshell'? It means 'in few words' or 'a summary'. A nutshell is very tiny, so very little can fit in it. We are going to learn to summarise what we've read. So, imagine when you are summarising that you are trying to fit your words into a nutshell.*

2. **Questions to ask for familiar fiction:**

   • *Who were the main characters?* • *How was the setting important in the story?* • *Who was telling the story? A character or a narrator?* • *Which part of the story did you like best?* • *Read the blurb on the back cover. Is the blurb a summary?* No, because it doesn't give the ending or all of the story events. A good blurb should make you want to read the book.

3. **Questions to ask for familiar non-fiction:**

   • *What was the text about?* • *Were there chapter headings, headings and sub-headings that helped you to know what you were reading about?* • *Who would the information be useful for?* • *Could you easily understand what the information was about?* • *Can you select the ten most important words from the text? Why did you choose them?*

There is no need to ask every question for every session.

4. **Say:** *Now, can you summarise the book using your own words?*

Key checks: Can pupils identify the main ideas in a text? Can they use their own words to summarise?

Extension: Ask pupils to write their responses to the questions. Pupils write a blurb in under 50 words.

Support: Scaffold answers for pupils by providing them with a checklist of things to include in their summaries.

How does it look?

Strand: Reading – comprehension

Learning objective: To identify how language, structure and presentation contribute to meaning.

You will need: a set of books carefully matched to pupils' reading ability (e.g. guided reading books or an article from a newspaper or printed from a website), two similar texts to compare (e.g. two sets of instructions)

1. **Say:** *We are going to discuss the 'shape' of a text in order to decide how it is fit for its purpose. We will do this by exploring the language, structure (that is, the chapters, beginning, middle, end, how paragraphs are grouped together) and presentation (the size of letters, font used, how the words are arranged on the page).*

2. **Questions to discuss structure:**

   - *How are the different sections of the story/text made clear?*

   - *Is the story straightforward? How has the structure of the book been organised to support this? For example, a book where a character is having flashbacks may be organised with alternating chapters of the flashback, then the present.*

   - *How are the different sections of the information made clear? Are you able to locate information quickly?*

3. **Questions to discuss presentation:**

   - *Here are two instructional texts. Is one presented more clearly than the other?*

   - *Does the presentation of this text make you want to read it? Why?*

   - *Has the author used the best layout?*

   - *Why did the author use bullet points/subheadings/a pie chart?*

4. **Questions to discuss language:**

   - *Who is the information for? Are there word choices that support this idea?*

   - *Has the writer made appropriate word choices?*

   - *How could the words be changed to make this suitable for pupils in Reception to understand?*

Key checks: Do pupils understand the difference between language, structure and presentation? Can they identify different text types? Are pupils talking about their opinions and using features of the text to support their ideas? For example, *Yes, the writer has made appropriate word choices, because he has used the word ecstatic to show happiness. A younger child may not understand this word, and I would change it to delighted.*

Extension: Compare more than two similar texts and comment about the language, structure and presentation.

Support: Provide pupils with a simple sentence starter to help them start their answer. *I think…* Help pupils to compile a list of different key organisational features and key words to help them in the discussion.

Find that fact

trand: Reading – comprehension

earning objective: To retrieve and record information from non-fiction.

ou will need: a set of non-fiction books/texts carefully matched to pupils' ading ability (e.g. guided non-fiction reading books or an article from a ewspaper or printed from a website – ideally the texts would be linked to a assroom topic), a set of fact-finding questions matched to the book (e.g. What ar was the first exploration of space? Which countries have sent people into ace?), writing books and pencils

ote: Pupils should have read the text at least once so they are able to read the xt fluently.

Say: *The purpose of information books is to provide information, and they should be organised in a way that helps us do this.*

Ask: *How do non-fiction texts support us to find information quickly?* Pupils should be able to refer to the contents and index pages and how these are set out (e.g. alphabetical or page order, columns).

Ask: *What if the question you are trying to answer doesn't include a word that is in the contents or index pages? How would you know where to look? Perhaps you want to find out if Bronze Age Man had discovered fire, but the book does not list 'fire' in the index page. How could you quickly look?* Pupils may suggest they flick quickly through the book, particularly the Bronze Age section.

Questions to ask about non-fiction:

- *What does the table/graph/pie chart show?*

- *What information can you get from the picture?*

- *Is there a fact box that organises information? For example, key dates?*

- *How do you scan the page to find information? Do you look at the diagrams and pictures first? The headings and subheadings or scan the text?*

Say: *Let's play 'Find that fact!' I'm going to ask some questions and you have to try and find the information as quickly and efficiently as you can.* Pupils write their answers to the questions in their books, or on printed question sheets. **Say:** *Remember to use all the skills we have talked about so far to find the answers to the questions.*

Key checks: Do pupils look in different parts of the book in order to find the answer? Are pupils using features of the book to support them (contents, index, glossary, fact boxes, headings and subheadings, labelled diagrams, photographs etc.)?

Extension: Ask pupils how they found the information. Record which feature of the book supported them. Ask pupils an open question, for example, **Ask:** *What was the most surprising fact you found?*

Support: Next to each question, a choice of two page numbers could be indicated. For example, **Say:** *What year was the first exploration of space? Will you find the answer on page 12 or page 16?* Pupils should look at the contents or index page to decide which page is more likely to answer their question.

Everybody talks, everybody listens

Strand: Reading – comprehension

Learning objective: To participate in discussion about books that are read to them and books they can read for themselves, taking turns and listening to what others say.

You will need: a set of books carefully matched to the pupils' reading ability (e.g. guided reading books or a class story book), lollipop sticks with pupils' names on them (optional)

Note: This objective will be repeated many times during the year. It will be continually assessed as the activities about reading comprehension are completed.

1. **Ask:** *Why do we need to listen to each other?* Allow pupils time to discuss, and take their feedback. **Say:** *We need to know what other people have said, so our discussion can build. Otherwise, we may repeat what has already been said, or miss out on something important.*

2. **Say:** *Make sure that everyone is listening. Sometimes, I will ask for one or two of you to share your ideas, and I may not want you to put your hand up. I will pull out a lolly stick with a name on it, which will make sure everyone gets a turn.*

3. **Say:** *Let's read the book now.* Decide on the type of questions you want to ask the pupils, and refer to those activities. Practise discussions using think, pair, share techniques. Make sure talking buddies are carefully paired to ensure effective conversation.

Note: It is useful to develop a stop signal, so pupils know when to end conversations. For example, you could raise a hand. This should be used consistently so pupils get used to it and respond quickly.

4. In group discussion, you may select a lollipop stick, and then direct questions to certain pupils or pairs. **Say:** _____, *could you share the idea you discussed with your partner? I think* _____ *may have said something similar.* _____, *was there anything else you would like to add to make the explanation clearer? I like the way the group are listening to each other, you're supporting each other to build ideas.*

Key checks: Are pupils taking turns to speak and to listen?

Extension: Can pupils build on each other's answers, referring to what others have said? (e.g. *I agree/disagree with what* _____ *said about* _____ *because...*)

Support: Support pupils in discussion using 'talk buddy', 'phone a friend' or 'revisit' techniques.

Higher homophones

Strand: Writing – transcription

Learning objective: To spell further homophones.

You will need: whiteboard, whiteboard pens and rubber, writing books and pencils

1. **Say:** *We are going to learn more about homophones. Can anyone tell me what a homophone is? Homophones are words that sound the same but look different.* **Ask:** *Can anyone think of an example?* (e.g. great/grate, see/sea)

2. **Say:** *I'm going to say a word that is a homophone. In pairs, can you think of both meanings of the word?* **Say:** *mist* (mist – a morning fog, missed – past tense of miss), *knot* (knot – a loop in rope, not – unable), *meat* (meat – food from animals, meet – to see someone and greet them), *peace* (peace – no fighting, piece – a chunk or part), *scene* (scene – an act in a play, seen – past tense of see).

3. **Say:** *Well done for knowing so many homophones, but here's the tricky bit, can you spell them? The words sound the same, but they are spelt differently.* Have pupils write and illustrate each word. Think of some spelling strategies to help.

4. **Say:** *We are going to have a spelling test with a difference. You need to listen to the word and its definition, so you write the correct homophone. Can you spell knot so it means 'tie a loop in rope'?* Continue with the spelling test.

Key checks: Do pupils understand what homophones are? Can pupils recognise a homophone? Do pupils know what both of the words mean? Can pupils link the correct spelling to the meaning? Can pupils use strategies to help them remember the homophones?

Extension: Continue to introduce further homophones, for example, reign/rain/rein, break/brake.

Support: Say: *Here is a sentence and two ways of spelling the missing word.* **Ask:** *How do I spell the missing word?* For example, write: We will _____ at the library. **Ask:** *Is it 'meet' or 'meat'?*

Plural possessives

Strand: Writing – transcription

Learning objective: To place the plural possessive apostrophe accurately in words with regular plurals and in words with irregular plurals.

You will need: whiteboard, whiteboard pen and rubber

1. **Say:** *We are going to use an apostrophe to show something belonging to a group. For example, a group of cyclists, a group of footballers, a group of boys. If something belongs to them, it is their possession, they* **possess** *it.* **Ask:** *What is an apostrophe? What does it look like? Where do I position it on the line?*

2. **Ask:** *What do cyclists possess?* Bikes. **Say:** *The bikes belong to the cyclists.* Write this on the whiteboard. Highlight the 's' that makes cyclists plural. **Say:** *Let's count the words in that sentence. There are six. We can use an apostrophe to show possession and to make the sentence shorter. Does anyone know how we can change the sentence using a possessive apostrophe? The cyclists' bikes.* Write this on the whiteboard. **Ask:** *How many words are there in this sentence? Three. How is this different to the singular possessive apostrophe: The cyclist's bikes.* Write this on the board. **Say:** *The apostrophe moves to come before the 's'. This meaning is now more than one bike belonging to just one cyclist.*

3. Write: 'The footballers shirts' on the whiteboard. **Ask:** *Where does the apostrophe go to show there are many footballers, each with one shirt?* Discuss the differences between: *The footballers' shirts* and *The footballer's shirts*.

4. Write: 'The boys cars' on the whiteboard. Repeat step 3.

5. Write: 'The childrens books' on the whiteboard. **Say:** *Children is an irregular plural because the word 'children' doesn't finish with 's'. The apostrophe goes before the 's' with an irregular plural.*

Key checks: Do pupils know how to form an apostrophe? Do they know where to place the plural possessive apostrophe? Do pupils understand the difference in meaning between *the cyclists' bikes* and *the cyclist's bikes*?

Extension: Ask pupils to use the possessive pronoun example within a sentence.

Support: Have the rules displayed on the whiteboard with examples, so pupils can see the difference between regular and irregular plural possessive pronouns. Show two examples of the same sentence with the apostrophe in different positions and guide pupils to understand which is correct and why.

Poor Pierre

Strand: Writing – transcription

Learning objective: To spell words that are often misspelt.

You will need: a puppet, a dictionary per pupil, flashcards with words incorrectly spelt (e.g. medicine (medisin), disappear (dissapear), through (throogh), separate (seperat)), or a piece of writing with spelling errors

1. **Say:** *Pierre the Puppet is having some difficulty with spelling and needs your help.* Show pupils the writing or flashcards. **Say:** *Some of these words don't look quite right.* **Ask:** *What can we use to check the spelling?* (a dictionary)

2. Model your thought process aloud as you look up the first word in the dictionary, for example 'dissapear.' **Say:** *The first letter is 'd' so, I need to look in the 'd' section. I know that 'd' is close to the front of the dictionary, after 'c'. Now I need to skim the page to see if the words start with 'di'. If I look at the last word, that tells me if I need to turn over. Now I need to look for words with 'dis'. Still skimming, but I'm going to scan each word more closely now until I find it.* Ask pupils to write the correct spelling of the word and to compare it to the misspelt word.

3. **Say:** *Choose a word you are going to check. Can you find it in the dictionary?* Ask each pupil to tell you the word they are looking for. When they find the word in the dictionary, they should write the correct spelling and compare it with the misspelt word.

4. Repeat with more words.

Key checks: Do pupils know the order of the alphabet? Can they accurately write the correct spelling of the misspelt word?

Extension: Ask pupils to improve the piece of writing or find synonyms by using a thesaurus. **Say:** *A thesaurus gives different words that have the same meaning. Using a thesaurus stops the same word being repeated, and helps give ideas for words that are repeated.* Select a word for pupils to improve (e.g. nice).

Support: Mark particular pages within the dictionary with post-it notes, so pupils can find them more quickly. Also point out the alphabet that commonly runs down the side of each page. Use a larger print dictionary if required, but ensure it contains the words you will be focusing on.

Decisive dictation

Strand: Writing – transcription

Learning objective: To write from memory simple sentences, dictated by the teacher, that include words and punctuation taught so far.

You will need: whiteboards, whiteboard pens and rubbers, or writing books and pencils, dictation sentences to include commonly misspelt words (underlined), e.g.:

Simple sentences: • The <u>guard</u> walked in a <u>circle</u>. • It was <u>difficult</u> to cut the <u>fruit</u>.

Longer sentences: • It will be very <u>difficult</u> to get off this <u>desert</u> island. • The <u>group</u> were very busy making tools like <u>early</u> man.

Longer sentences with tricky punctuation: • "Let's continue to the <u>right</u>," said dad. • "I'll be ready in a <u>minute</u> Mum!" Linda answered.

1. **Say:** *I am going to dictate a sentence, and I would like you to write down the exact words I say.* **Say:** *The guard walked in a circle.*

2. Repeat the sentence.

3. **Say:** *Now it's your turn to say the sentence.*

4. **Say:** *Repeat the sentence one more time.*

5. **Say:** *Now write the sentence on your whiteboard.*

6. **Say:** *Let's check your sentence.*

7. **Ask:** *Have you written each word? Have you spelt all the words correctly? Have you remembered to start with a capital letter and finish with a full stop?*

Key checks: Are pupils repeating the sentence exactly? Are they able to spell all the words correctly?

Extension: Select longer sentences.

Support: Select simple sentences. Have just one word from the tricky spelling list (e.g. *It was hard to cut the <u>fruit</u>*).

Sharpen your style

Strand: Writing – transcription

Learning objective: To use the diagonal and horizontal strokes that are needed to join letters and understand which letters, when adjacent to one another, are best left unjoined to increase the legibility, consistency and quality of their handwriting.

Note: You will need to follow your school's handwriting policy.

You will need: pencils, paper, handwriting paper

1. **Say:** *When you are writing, you should usually join your letters. But you don't need to join all your letters. 'r' can be confused with 'n' if you join it, and we don't join capital letters.*

2. **Say:** *Let's start to develop your own style.*

3. **Ask:** *Can you write these words: was, will, you, stop, sharp? Write all the letters in lowercase. Practise writing each word more than once.*

4. **Ask:** *Can you write these sentences? Practise writing each sentence as quickly and neatly as you can, making sure you have your ascenders and descenders as similarly sized as possible. Remember to start with a capital letter.* Dictate the following sentences:

   • *A prince went on a quest.*

   • *In a green forest far away grows a rare plant.*

5. **Say:** *When you are writing, the space you leave between each word only needs to be about the size of an 'o'. Let's write the following sentences, leaving only a small space between each word. Dictate the sentences:*

   • *It grows high in the tops of trees, close to sunlight.*

   • *Once a year, it produces fiery bright flowers.*

6. **Say:** *Let's look at each other's books. Can you see how we have all written the same sentences, but everyone's handwriting is slightly different? I can tell this is _____ writing because the letters are quite rounded.*

Key checks: Are pupils forming their letters using correct formation?

Extension: Pupils think of their own sentences to write. Make sure they are using a joined style – it can be easy to forget when they are thinking about what to write.

Support: Pupils should be forming unjoined letters using the correct formation, so they may need to work on these individually first.

Analyse this

Strand: Writing – composition

Learning objective: To discuss writing similar to that which they are planning to write in order to understand and learn from its structure, vocabulary and grammar.

You will need: Copies of a finished piece of writing (e.g. if you are going to be writing an adventure story, use an adventure story), highlighter pens, different coloured post-it notes for different word classes, pencils

1. **Say:** *We are going to read this piece of writing and choose ideas we want to use in our own writing.* **Ask:** *What verbs has the author used?* As a group, highlight the verbs and discuss which are the most interesting and whether they could be replaced with more interesting ones (e.g. 'went' is not very interesting, 'wandered' is better).

2. **Say:** *Now choose some verbs you may like to use in your story and write them on a post-it note.*

3. **Say:** *Now highlight the adjectives you feel add to the mood of the story.* Pupils should highlight interesting adjectives in the text. **Say:** *Choose the adjectives you may like to use in your story and write them on a post-it note.*

4. **Say:** *Has the author used any similes in this piece of writing? These will help us compare something we don't know to something we do know.* Pupils highlight any examples of similes. **Say:** *Now choose the similes you may like to use in your story and write them on a post-it note.*

5. **Ask:** *Has the author used any direct speech?* Pupils highlight direct speech. **Ask:** *Are there any ideas you can use?*

6. **Ask:** *What punctuation has the author used? Can you make your own punctuation bank? Take a post-it note and write the punctuation you can see on it. You only need one example of each.*

Key checks: Can the pupils find examples of each element of writing?

Extension: If there are no similes in the extract, can the pupils think of a suitable one to add? Pupils review, select and mark the most effective word choice on each post-it note and explain why. They then use this word choice in a sentence.

Support: Offer pupils a choice of words (e.g. 'racing' and 'windy'). **Ask:** *Can you choose the verb/adjective?*

Plan the perfect piece

Strand: Writing – composition

Learning objective: To plan a piece of writing.

You will need: paper and pencils, the post-it notes from the 'Analyse this' activity either a prepared story mountain template or other story plan, thesauruses

Note: Writing will ideally be linked to a class theme or topic.

1. **Say:** *The best pieces of writing are carefully planned and created. We are going to create a story plan that will help us to write a story about…*

2. **Ask:** *Before you start, who will be reading this story?* Allow pupils a short time to think, and take their feedback. **Say:** *So, the story will be written for children. Now, can you write some words or phrases to describe the setting? What would you be able to see, hear, smell, touch?* Write words or phrases that pupils suggest on a story plan on the whiteboard. Pupils should also look at their post-it notes from the previous session for any adjectives they would like to use and begin to create their own story plan.

3. **Say:** *Who will the characters be? Do you want your main character to be an adult or a child? Animal or human?* Allow pupils time to discuss and take feedback. Add this information to the story plan. **Say:** *You will need two characters to have a conversation, so who else will feature in your story?* Add this information to the plan

4. **Say:** *Now we need to decide on the order of events in the story.* Write key words onto the story plan. **Say:** *Are there any brilliant verbs you wrote that you would like to use? Which verbs will you use to show how your character moves? Let's write these down.*

5. **Say:** *What would your characters have a conversation about? Let's decide where in the story this would go.* Write this information on the story plan.

6. Encourage pupils to add any more detail they would like to their own versions of the story plan.

Key checks: Can pupils create a detailed story plan? Are they noting all their ideas down and keeping up?

Extension: Encourage pupils to use a thesaurus to find different examples of verbs or adjectives. For example, look up 'move' to find movement verbs. Look up 'high' to find other adjectives.

Support: Provide more structure on the plan by having areas to complete and bullet points. Write some words on a whiteboard for pupils to choose from.

Superior sentences

Learning objective: To draft and write by composing and rehearsing sentences orally (including dialogue), progressively building a varied and rich vocabulary and an increasing range of sentence structures (English Appendix 2).

You will need: story plans from the 'Plan the perfect piece' session, pencils, paper, whiteboard, whiteboard pen and rubber

1. **Say:** *Do you remember our story plan? Well, today we are going to think about different sentence types and joining words to use to write our story.*

2. **Say:** *I'm going to practise my first sentence out loud. I want to introduce my main characters and describe them a little bit. Then I want to say where they are and what they are doing.* Demonstrate how to say each sentence out loud before writing it. **Ask:** *What will your first sentence be?* **Say:** *Look at your story plan and say it out loud. Now write your sentence.*

3. **Say:** *I need to look at my story plan to see what happens next. This is an exciting part of the story and there is a lot of detail, so I am going to use conjunctions to join my sentences together. I think in this next sentence, I'm going to show off that I can use subordinate conjunctions* (so, while, when, because, before, after). **Ask:** *Which conjunction are you going to use?* **Say:** *Look at your story plan and write your sentence.*

4. **Say:** *I am going to check my story plan again. It looks like I want to have a conversation between my two characters now. Here are the verbs I want to include to show how they are speaking.* **Ask:** *How are your characters going to speak? What did you write on your story plan?*

5. Continue explaining your thoughts about the writing process, modelling sentences aloud, and asking pupils to write their version. If using this writing for the next activity, do not include paragraphs.

Key checks: Can pupils use the process of orally rehearsing a sentence before writing? Provide a differentiated success criteria of what they should include so they can tick things off to support their self-assessment.

Extension: Pupils write their own sentences without prompting, using the story plan for support. Write the success criteria: simile, inverted commas, possessive apostrophe, adverbs, subordinate clause, conjunction. Pupils rub these out when they have used them.

Support: Pupils may need to write simple sentences based on their story plan, and read through with adult support, joining some of the sentences using conjunctions.

Progressive paragraphs

Strand: Writing – composition

Learning objective: To organise paragraphs around a theme.

You will need: a piece of writing (e.g. the writing completed in the last activity if it is suitable), pencil and paper, coloured pencil

1. **Say:** *To organise a piece of writing, authors use paragraphs to make their writing easier to read.* **Ask:** *What is a paragraph?* Allow pupils time to discuss. **Say:** *A paragraph is a collection of sentences that all develop the same single idea.*

2. **Say:** *Let's look at the writing you completed in the last session. Each paragraph should be about a different idea. Draw two forward slashes to show where the first paragraph should end.*

3. **Ask:** *What is the next paragraph about?* Allow pupils time to discuss. **Say:** *Here you have stopped describing the main character and you are describing the setting, so this is a new paragraph.*

4. **Ask:** *What is the next paragraph about?* Allow pupils time to discuss. **Say:** *It is where there is a change in idea. Here, your main character has met another character.*

Key checks: Do pupils understand how a paragraph develops an idea? Can pupils find where paragraphs should begin and end?

Extension: Pupils write an extra paragraph.

Support: Guide pupils by reading the text out together and allowing extra time for thinking.

Creative characters, special settings, pleasing plots

Strand: Writing – composition

Learning objective: To create settings, characters and plot.

You will need: thesaurus, paper and pencil, magazines or books

1. **Say:** *We are going to create all the elements for a super story. We will create a character, design the setting and decide what happens. Let's start by deciding on our character. What sort of character shall we have?* Look through the magazines and books for ideas. Allow pupils time to select their character. Pupils may want character traits from a few different characters to create their own.

2. **Say:** *Now you have chosen your character, you need to describe him/her in detail.* **Ask:** *What does he/she look like? What sort of clothes does he/she wear? Age? Family? Do they have things in a bag or pocket? What sort of person are they? Kind/unkind? The more we know about them, the easier our story will be to write.* Pupils write notes using bullet points under the subheadings appearance, personality, family, possessions, interests/skills.

3. **Ask:** *At the start of the story, where will your character be? At their house? In the woods or mountains? Let's describe the setting. What is the weather like? What will the character see and hear? How do they feel in this place?* Pupils write notes about their setting using bullet points.

4. **Say:** *We now have two out of three elements in place for our story. Next we need to plan what will happen. Your character could go on a journey, but get lost on the way. They need a reason to go on the journey.* **Ask:** *Is the character going to visit a friend? Buy something from a shop? What will happen on their journey?* Pupils write notes about their plot. They could do this on a story mountain.

5. **Say:** *Finally, you need to decide how your character will reach their destination.* **Ask:** *Will another character come and help? Will there be a sign to help them find their way?* Pupils write notes about the resolution to their story. They could do this on a story mountain.

Key checks: Can pupils make decisions about their character, setting and plot? Can pupils use lots of interesting vocabulary to describe the character and setting?

Extension: Use a thesaurus to support pupils to find more interesting vocabulary.

Support: Divide the session into smaller sessions to deliver character, setting and plot separately. Pupils could work collaboratively, contributing ideas to the same character, setting and plot.

Organising information

Strand: Writing – composition

Learning objective: To use simple organisational devices: headings and subheadings in non-narrative material.

Note: This session would be most meaningful if linked to a classroom topic or theme.

You will need: paper and pencils, whiteboards, whiteboard pens and rubbers, post-it notes

1. **Say:** *We are going to write a leaflet about after-school clubs at our school.* **Ask:** *Can you make a list of activities that happen at our school? Write each one on a post-it note.*

2. **Ask:** *What would be a good title for the leaflet?* (e.g. After-school activities at _____ Primary) **Say:** *How could we organise the activities in our leaflet? What would the categories be?* (e.g. sports, music, art... or indoor activities, outdoor activities) **Say:** *These will be our headings. Write these at the top of your whiteboards.*

3. **Ask:** *Can you sort the activities under the headings? Stick the post-it notes under the correct heading. If an activity could be under more than one heading you may need to revise the headings.* Allow pupils time to arrange their post-it notes and to review the headings.

4. **Ask:** *What would people reading the leaflet want to know about after-school activities?* (e.g. who runs the club, what time it happens, where it happens, who can go, what you do there) **Say:** *Each club needs to have the same information.* Make a list of what should be included on a whiteboard. These will become the success criteria.

5. **Ask:** *Can you pick a club to write about? Have you included all the information? Have you used subheadings?* Ask each pupil to write one or two sections each. **Say:** *Write on small pieces of paper so we can arrange the finished sections.*

6. When all the sections have been written, **Ask:** *How should we organise the information?* Organise the information under headings, subheadings and, additionally, by time of year or age group.

Key checks: Can pupils sort information in a logical way?

Extension: Pupils write individual leaflets.

Support: Have the points to include on a template for pupils to complete, rather than writing their own paragraph.

Have I missed anything?

trand: Writing – composition

earning objective: To evaluate and edit by: assessing the effectiveness of their wn and others' writing and suggesting improvements.

ou will need: The completed leaflet about after-school clubs from 'Organising formation' success criteria list, coloured pencils, pencil, paper

Ask: *Can you read through the success criteria list? What does it mean?*
Say: *It means you need to make sure your piece of writing includes every point on that list.*

Ask: *Can you check through one of your paragraphs and make sure it includes every point? Use colouring pencils to colour code the success criteria. For example, who runs the club, underline in blue. Where it takes place, underline in yellow. If pupils are missing some information,* **Say:** *Well done for noticing you forgot that bit. Where can you add it in?*

Say: *Now swap one of your paragraphs with someone else on the table. They are going to use the success criteria to check it. Follow the same colour code to check your partner's work.*

Ask: *Can you let the person know what they did well first? After that, let them know if they missed anything.*

Ask: *Are there any words in your description of the activity that you think could be improved? Can you use a thesaurus?*

---

ey checks: Do pupils understand that they need to include everything on the uccess criteria list? Can pupils find examples of each element listed in the uccess criteria in their writing? Can pupils read each other's writing?

xtension: n/a

upport: In pairs, pupils find what is being asked for together. If pupils require a t of support, make a large photocopy of the leaflet and ask them in turn to find e example you have asked for on the group leaflet and highlight it. **Ask:** *Does verybody agree?* If not, **Ask:** *Can you explain why you disagree?*

Pronoun puzzle

Strand: Writing – composition

Learning objective: To improve sentences with the accurate use of pronouns.

You will need: one piece of writing requiring editing or the sample piece below per pupil, coloured pens, writing pencils, a whiteboard, a whiteboard pen

> Pete was riding Pete's bike to school. Pete was just getting to the gate when Pete met up with Kimmy, who was pushing Kimmy's scooter. Pete and Kimmy nearly collided, but Pete braked hard. "Wow that was close," Pete said. Kimmy scooted through and made Kimmy's way up to the bike shed. Pete followed and soon Ling and Kasper arrived. The friends parked up the bikes and scooters and walked around to class. Pete, Kimmy, Ling and Kasper's teacher opened the door and Pete, Kimmy, Ling and Kasper rushed in.

1. Read the piece of writing out loud.

2. **Say:** *Using the children's names all the time makes the writing very repetitive. We can replace their names with pronouns.* **Ask:** *Do you know what a pronoun is? Can you write any on your boards? What is a pronoun?* Allow pupils time to think, and take their feedback. **Say:** *A pronoun is a word that replaces a proper noun or name. For example, he/her/she/his.* **Ask:** *Can you find and underline the proper nouns in the text? What could we use to replace them?*

3. Work together to replace some of the names in the text with pronouns and reread the finished piece.

4. **Ask:** *Did we change every proper noun into a pronoun? No? Why not?* **Say:** *Because if we did then we wouldn't understand who is being talked about. We only use pronouns to avoid repetition in our writing.*

Key checks: Do pupils know what a proper noun is? Do pupils know what a pronoun is? Do they know which proper nouns need to change?

Extension: Give pupils a longer piece of writing to edit. Include some red herrings, like 'there' instead of 'their' or misused pronouns, like 'she' instead of 'her'.

Support: Make a list of pronouns on a whiteboard together. Pupils can use this to identify pronouns in their work.

Spot the mistakes

?arning objective: To proof-read a piece of writing for spelling and punctuation rors.

?u will need: one piece of writing requiring editing per pupil, or use the sample ?ece below, coloured pens, writing pencils

---

Georgie and alex went to their guitar leson a littel worried. They had forgotten ?heir guitar music, agane. What do you think he will say, muttered Alex They ?eedn't have worried through. Mr Rawlings taught them to plai hot cross buns. ?om memory

---

Ensure each pupil has a piece of writing. Read the piece of writing out loud as pupils read to themselves.

Ask: *Does it all make sense? Are any words spelt incorrectly?* Focus the spelling check on words that have been learnt in class. Pupils correct the misspelt words on their own sample.

Ask: *Are there any problems with the punctuation? Let's check the start and end of sentences first.* Model how to check a piece of text and correct on the board. Pupils then check and amend their own sample text using a coloured pen.

Say: *Now let's check for the correct use of capital letters.* Model how to check and correct. Pupils then check and amend their own sample text.

Say: *Finally, it sounded like there was a question word. That would mean we need a question mark. Where should it go?* Pupils then check and amend their own sample.

?orrected version: Georgie and Alex went to their guitar lesson a little worried. They had forgotten their guitar music, again. "What do you think he will say?" muttered Alex. They needn't have worried though. Mr Rawlings taught them to play *Hot Cross Buns* from memory.

?y checks: Can pupils recognise and correct spelling and punctuation errors?

?tension: Give pupils a longer piece of writing to edit.

?pport: Give pupils a word bank, which includes misspelt words from the ?ssage. Pupils use this as a reference when spell checking independently. Tell ?m how many punctuation errors there are.

Read it out

Strand: Writing – composition

Learning objective: To read aloud their own writing using appropriate intonation and expression.

You will need: an edited, improved and proof-read piece of writing from each pupil

1. **Say:** *You're going to read out a story you have written.*

   Note: If a pupil feels a little nervous, they may wish to read aloud to a smaller group, rather than a larger group or the whole class.

2. **Ask:** *Can you read your story to yourself? As you read, make sure you are reading all your improvements. Can you use different voices where you have characters speaking?*

3. **Say:** *I am going to read my story out loud. I would like you to listen carefully and give me two stars and a wish when I've finished.* Read some parts of the story in a monotonous voice, without any pauses or breaks. **Ask:** *Can you give me two stars and a wish?* Encourage pupils to refer to the fact that you didn't use interesting intonation, tone and volume. Read the story again, showing that you have listened to the pupils and have improved your reading aloud.

4. **Say:** *Now read your work aloud to a critical friend before sharing with the group.*

5. Following the reading, offer praise first, and only one point for development.

Key checks: Can pupils read their own writing using appropriate intonation, tone and volume? Are pupils remembering to incorporate suggested improvements when re-reading?

Extension: Pupils could read to a different year group.

Support: Pupils rehearse with an adult, before reading to a group.

Sunny subordinates

Strand: Writing – vocabulary, grammar and punctuation

Learning objectives: To extend the range of sentences with more than one clause by using a wider range of conjunctions, including when, if, because, although; to join sentences using subordinate conjunctions.

You will need: whiteboard, whiteboard pen and rubber, writing books and pencils, conjunctions written on a whiteboard or on separate cards, strips of paper and scissors

1. **Say:** *To make our writing more interesting, we should include single-clause sentences and multi-clause sentences. Conjunctions are used to join clauses.*

2. **Ask:** *Do you know any subordinate conjunctions?* (when, if, because, although) Write suggestions on the board and add any of the four that pupils do not suggest. **Ask:** *Which conjunction would you use to join the two clauses...: The ice-cream started to melt _____ the sun came out from behind a cloud?*

3. **Say:** *Let's test all four of the subordinating conjunctions. Which one sounds best?* Ask various pupils to read the sentence aloud with one of the four subordinate conjunctions in the gap. (*because* and *when* both make sense)

4. **Say:** *Look at the two clauses of the sentence we have just created. 'The ice-cream started to melt' is the main clause. It makes sense on its own.*

5. **Ask:** *Which is the main and which is the subordinate clause for this sentence?* Write on the whiteboard: When it's a sunny day, people seem to smile more. The subordinate clause starts with 'when', a subordinate conjunction.

Key checks: Do pupils understand what a subordinate conjunction is?

Extension: Give pupils further sentences and ask them to use subordinate conjunctions that they haven't used already, for example 'until', 'while' or 'even though'. Pupils explore moving the position of the subordinate clause to the front and end of the main clause to see the effect on the sentence/reader.

Support: Have a sentence written along a thin strip of paper and support pupils to cut the sentence where the clauses meet then rearrange the order. Pupils then write their own sentence using the example and repeat cutting and rearranging.

Changing tenses

Strand: Writing – vocabulary, grammar and punctuation

Learning objective: To use the present perfect form of verbs in contrast to the past tense.

You will need: whiteboards, whiteboard pens and rubbers, writing books and pencils

1. **Say:** *The present perfect tense is used to talk or write about actions that started in the past but are still happening now. It uses 'have' and the verb with an –ed suffix if it is a regular verb, although there are some exceptions. An example with a regular verb is: I have lived in my house for six years.*

2. **Ask:** *Which other tense uses verbs with an –ed ending?* The simple past tense. **Ask:** *When do you use the simple past tense?* Allow pupils time to think and take feedback. **Say:** *The simple past tense is used to talk about actions that have been completed. For example, I danced at the disco.*

3. Write: 'have/has + verb with –ed suffix (for regular verbs)' on the whiteboard. **Say:** *This is how we make the present perfect.*

4. **Ask:** *How can I change this sentence written in the simple past tense into the present perfect tense? 'Grandad worked at the shoe factory.'* Allow pupils time to think, and take their feedback. ('Grandad has worked at the shoe factory.')

    Say: *When we use the present perfect tense, it is because the action is still happening or is still important, so it makes more sense to say how long the action has been happening for. In the case of Grandad and the shoe factory, let's add 'all his life' to the sentence: 'Grandad has worked at the shoe factory all his life.'*

5. **Ask:** *How can I change this sentence written in the simple past tense into the present perfect tense? 'I walked two miles.'* (I have walked two miles.)

    Say: *Do you think the person has stopped walking or is still walking? It sounds as though they are still walking or have only just stopped. What about in the past tense? Yes, the person stopped walking some time in the past.* Draw a time line to represent these two actions. Draw a stick person walking on each tense.

6. **Say:** *Let's play a game. Each person will think of their own 'Who has…?' questions using the present perfect tense. Everybody else will write their answer on their whiteboard. For example: Who has seen a famous person? Who has eaten and enjoyed Brussels sprouts? Remember to answer the*

94

*questions using the present perfect tense. I have seen a famous person, or
I have not seen a famous person.* At the end of the game, check that pupils
have spotted the irregular past participles.

Ask: *Can you say which tense should be used to complete the sentence I am
writing on the board?* Write:

- The girl _____ to school yesterday. (walk)

- I have _____ at this school for three years. (be)

- Dave _____ to his dog to come back. (call)

---

ey checks: Do pupils understand the difference between the simple past tense
nd the present perfect tense?

xtension: Extend understanding beyond first- and third-person singular into
ural, e.g. we have sat still for hours/they have eaten their dinner.

upport: Answer questions as a group and model writing the answer. Pupils
rite in their books at the same time as adult modelling on whiteboard.

Noun or pronoun?

Strand: Writing – vocabulary, grammar and punctuation

Learning objective: To choose a noun or pronoun to avoid repetition in writing.

You will need: a piece of writing produced by a pupil, or use the sample below, coloured pens, whiteboard, whiteboard pen and rubber

---

The squirrel ran up the tree to a small shadow. The squirrel darted inside and Ashley could hear rustling. The squirrel poked its head out of the hole and then scurried back down the tree. Ashley watched the squirrel return to the base of the tree and briefly dig. The squirrel unearthed another walnut, just as Ashley sneezed. The squirrel froze. Ashley sneezed again and the squirrel dashed back up the tree, like a blur.

---

1. **Ask:** *What is a noun?* **Say:** *A noun is a naming word. It may be an object, or a name or a person or place.*

2. **Ask:** *What is a pronoun?* **Say:** *A pronoun can replace the noun in a sentence. Examples include she, he, they, his, her, we, their.*

3. Read and display the piece of writing. **Ask:** *What do you think? Can you give two stars and a wish?* For example, stars could be given for capital letters, interesting adjectives, use of inverted commas, joined up handwriting. Encourage pupils to make the writing less repetitive by replacing the nouns with a pronoun.

4. **Say:** *Let's use our coloured pens to change nouns to pronouns. Which ones should we change? All of them or some of them?* Allow pupils to test using the piece of writing:

The squirrel ran up the tree to a small shadow. It darted inside and Ashley could hear rustling. The squirrel poked its head out of the hole and then scurried back down the tree. Ashley watched the squirrel return to the base of the tree and briefly dig. It unearthed another walnut, just as Ashley sneezed. The squirrel froze. She sneezed again and the squirrel dashed back up the tree, like a blur.

---

5. **Say:** *So, introduce the noun first, then use pronouns to stop the writing from sounding too repetitive.*

Key checks: Do pupils know what a noun is? Do pupils know what a pronoun is?

Extension: Ask pupils to revisit a piece of their own writing and edit it for pronouns.

Support: Highlight the nouns that need to be changed in the piece of writing and provide a pronoun bank (pronouns written on a whiteboard).

Joining sentences

Strand: Writing – vocabulary, grammar and punctuation

Learning objective: To use conjunctions to express time and cause.

You will need: whiteboards, whiteboard pens and rubbers, writing books and pencils. Prepare the following sentences:

- Lottie was excited for the weekend because it was her birthday.

- Susie was at the swimming pool with her friends when she realised she had left her swimming bag at home.

- Jamal caught the Frisbee easily although he found catching a ball tricky.

1. **Ask:** *What is a conjunction?* **Say:** *A conjunction is a word that joins two clauses to make a longer sentence. Conjunctions can tell us about passing time, for example, when, since, yet. They can also tell us why – express cause – using 'because'.*

2. Show pupils the prepared sentences. **Say:** *Write the conjunction in each sentence on your whiteboard.* **Ask:** *Is it a conjunction of time or cause?*

3. **Say:** *Write the conjunctions when, although, because, until on your whiteboard. You are going to use each one in a sentence.*

4. Read out some gapped sentences. Pupils write the missing conjunction.

   - *Danny wanted sausages with his potatoes (until) the dinner lady dropped the last one on the floor.*

   - *Becky had to go on the bus to work (because) her usual train had been cancelled.*

   - *Flora said she hated peas (although) she had never actually tried them!*

   - *Wesley thought he was going to be waiting at the bus stop for another half an hour (when) his friend drove by and gave him a lift.*

Key checks: Do pupils understand the purpose of conjunctions?

Extension: Pupils write their own sentence using the conjunction 'since', which was not used in the original activity.

Support: Have two sentences prepared with only the conjunction differing. Pupils can then choose the sentence that sounds right. For example: Becky had to go on the bus to work <u>when</u> her usual train had been cancelled. Becky had to go on the bus to work <u>because</u> her usual train had been cancelled.

Adverbials to the front!

Strand: Writing – vocabulary, grammar and punctuation

Learning objective: To use fronted adverbials and commas after them.

You will need: whiteboards, whiteboard pens and rubbers, strips of paper with the extension activity phrases on them, highlighter pens, writing books and pencils

1. **Ask:** *What is an adverbial phrase?* **Say:** *Phrases are a group of words. Adverbial phrases are groups of words that answer the questions how?, where?, when? or why?* Write how?, where?, when? and why? on the board.

2. **Say:** *The lambs were being fed.* **Ask:** *When were they being fed? This morning, the lambs were being fed. Write the adverbial phrase on your whiteboard.* (This morning)

3. **Say:** *The lambs were being fed.* **Ask:** *How were they being fed? The lambs were being fed using gigantic baby bottles. Write the adverbial phrase on your whiteboard.* (using gigantic baby bottles)

4. **Say:** *The lambs were being fed.* **Ask:** *Where were they being fed? The lambs were being fed in the new barn. Write the adverbial phrase on your whiteboard.* (in the new barn)

5. **Say:** *The lambs were being fed.* **Ask:** *Why were they being fed? The lambs were being fed because they were new born. Write the adverbial phrase on your whiteboard.* (because they were new born)

6. **Say:** *A fronted adverbial phrase is simply an adverbial phrase at the start of the sentence. Re-write the sentences about where and why the lambs were being fed as fronted adverbial sentences on your whiteboard. It should be followed by a comma, then the rest of the sentence.*

Key checks: Do pupils know what an adverbial phrase is? Can they identify and give examples?

Extension: Ask pupils to re-write other sentences as fronted adverbial sentences. For example: We went to the park yesterday. (Yesterday, we went to the park.)

Support: Write sentences used in the extension activity onto strips of paper. Highlight the adverbial phrases. Support pupils to write the fronted adverbial phrase, position the comma and write the rest of the sentence. You could do this by cutting the sentence and getting them to re-arrange it.

Talk the talk

Strand: Writing – vocabulary, grammar and punctuation

Learning objective: To use inverted commas to punctuate direct speech.

You will need: whiteboards, whiteboard pens and rubbers, writing books and pencils

1. **Ask:** *How do you recognise direct speech in a book?* Allow pupils time to think. **Say:** *There are inverted commas (speech marks) to show when a character is talking.* **Ask:** *Where are the inverted commas?* Allow pupils time to think. **Say:** *They hang in the sky above the line, in pairs, and they go either side of the direct speech.*

2. Draw a speech bubble around a sentence of direct speech on the whiteboard and pretend to pop it. Rub out the speech bubble, but leave small marks like inverted commas around the sentence. **Say:** *This sentence was inside the speech bubble. The parts of the bubble that are left now we have popped it go around the sentence like inverted commas. Inside the inverted commas, the sentence needs to start with a capital letter and end with punctuation.* **Ask:** *Can you show me some inverted commas on your whiteboards?*

3. **Ask:** *Can you write these sentences into your books, adding inverted commas in the correct place?*

   * Rik called please bring me a chocolate biscuit.

   * Tracey chuckled get that cat out of the box.

   * Benji muttered I really want our team to win.

4. **Say:** *Now let's check the sentences through together.* As you write, **Say:** *Capital R for Rik, called, comma, inverted commas to show the speech is starting. Now a capital P for please, (the rest of the sentence), finish with a full stop, because the whole sentence should be inside the inverted commas. Finally, add the other set of inverted commas.*

   * Rik called, "Please bring me a chocolate biscuit."

   * Tracey chuckled, "Get that cat out of the box."

   * Benji muttered, "I really want our team to win."

Key checks: Can pupils correctly position inverted commas? Are pupils correctly punctuating the direct speech?

Extension: Ask pupils to punctuate a sentence requiring punctuation other than a full stop at the end. For example, Where is my cup of tea asked Mrs Gill. "Where is my cup of tea?" asked Mrs Gill.

Support: Write the step-by-step process on the whiteboard: inverted commas, capital letter, sentence, punctuation, inverted commas. Model the example sentences in step 3 if required.

Who does this belong to?

Strand: Writing – vocabulary, grammar and punctuation

Learning objective: To use a possessive apostrophe with plural nouns.

You will need: whiteboard, whiteboard pens and rubbers, writing books and pencils

1. **Ask:** *What is a noun? Can you give me an example?* Allow pupils thinking time, and take their feedback. Pupils will most likely give a singular example, for example, chair or table. **Ask:** *Is this a singular or plural noun? Can you make this a plural noun?*

2. **Say:** *Plural nouns usually end with –s. Let's compare these sentences.*

   • The cushions on the chair.

   • The cushions on the chairs.

   In the first one, cushions is plural but chair is singular, so there is only one chair. In the second sentence, both cushions and chairs are plural. By using a possessive apostrophe, we can use fewer words and show that the cushions belong to the chair.

   • The chair's cushions.

   • The chairs' cushions.

3. **Ask:** *What is different about the position of the apostrophe in these sentences?* **Say:** *The first sentence is about one chair with cushions. It is one chair, so the apostrophe goes before the 's'. The second sentence is about lots of chairs, all with cushions. The apostrophe goes after the 's' because we are talking about lots of chairs.* Point to the position of the apostrophe as you are explaining.

4. **Ask:** *Can you add the possessive apostrophe to these sentences and make them shorter? Underline the plural nouns.*

The string on the kite.	The strings on the kites.
The food bowl for the cat.	The food bowls for the cats.
The books for the girl.	The books for the girls.
The frame for the photo.	The frames for the photos.

Solution:

The kite's string.	The kites' strings.
The cat's food bowl.	The cats' food bowls.
The girl's books.	The girls' books.
The photo's frame.	The photos' frames.

Key checks: Do pupils know what plural nouns are? Do pupils understand how to use the possessive apostrophe?

Extension: Tell pupils that some plural nouns are irregular – they do not finish with –s. For example, children, sheep. Irregular plural nouns follow the same rules as singular nouns. The children's toys.

Support: Ensure pupils are confidently using the possessive apostrophe for singular nouns. Give pupils lots of examples (singular from step 4) and ask them to write the phrases, correctly using an apostrophe.

Grammar galore

trand: Writing – vocabulary, grammar and punctuation

earning objective: To discuss reading and writing using the correct ammatical terms.

ou will need: examples of pupils' writing, reading books, post-it notes, pens or encils

ote: Pupils should talk about their writing and reading regularly. Encourage se of correct grammatical terms. Key vocabulary: preposition, conjunction, word mily, prefix, clause, subordinate clause, direct speech, consonant letter, vowel tter, inverted commas (or 'speech marks').

ou will need: examples of pupils' writing, reading books, post-it notes and pens ' pencils

Focus individually on a pupil's writing. **Ask:**

- *Can you tell me what punctuation you have used in this sentence?*

- *Why did you decide to use this punctuation mark?*

- *Does your sentence make sense? Re-read it and check.*

- *Have you used any words with prefixes?*

Focus on a section from a book pupils are reading. **Ask:**

- *Is that singular or plural?*

- *What is this punctuation mark called?*

- *Can you find a subordinate conjunction?*

- *Can you find a consonant letter?*

- *Can you find a vowel letter?*

---

ey checks: Are pupils using grammatical terms correctly and confidently?

xtension: Ask pupils to find examples of different grammatical features listed key vocabulary. Give them post-it notes to label features they find in reading ooks.

upport: Ensure pupils are confident using terminology from Year 2 (noun, noun rase, statement, question, exclamation, command, compound, suffix, adjective, verb, verb tense (past, present), apostrophe, comma).